Mountain Leadership

Eric Langmuir

The official handbook of the
Mountain Leadership Training Boards
of Great Britain and Northern Ireland

First published 1969; revised and reprinted 1973, reprinted 1976

Published by the Scottish Sports Council
1 St. Colme Street, Edinburgh EH3 6AA   Telephone: 031-225 8411

Contents

Foreword

This is a new and completely revised edition of Mountain Leadership. Again it has been prepared by the Scottish Mountain Leadership Training Board on behalf of the three Training Boards of the United Kingdom and is published by the Scottish Sports Council. Again the editor and principal author is Eric Langmuir to whom we are particularly grateful for his distinguished contribution not only to this official handbook of the Boards but, from the outset, to the whole field of mountain leadership training.

The handbook has been revised to take account of the changes in attitudes and practices in the field and of substantial amendments to the scheme since 1969. It is now not too much to say that mountain leadership training is established as the normal requirement for those taking parties of young people on to the hills. Along with comparable qualifications in the other major outdoor pursuits, a Mountain Leadership Certificate is seen as evidence of the minimum technical standard reasonably to be expected of those teachers, youth leaders or other adults who wish to accept responsibility for the care of young people in potentially hazardous situations on mountains. The basic Mountain Leadership Certificate, relevant to summer conditions only, does not demand a high standard of performance from a candidate but it does inevitably require a definite commitment in terms of time and application. After all, one does not become a competent mountain walker overnight and the mountain leader has to add a further vital dimension to his personal skills as a walker, the ability to care for a party at all times, a quality neither easy to acquire nor, for that matter, easy to assess.

So standards have to be set which recognise these factors and, at the same time, offer a practicable service to all potential leaders and their employers. The detailed arrangements involved have changed and will continue to do so with alterations not only to the 'summer' Certificate scheme but to its much more demanding counterpart for winter conditions. The literally enormous increase in demand for training at leadership level has, of itself, required greater provision for instructors to train and assess the leaders and for this reason, as well as because of the further rapid development of courses in outdoor education in schools and residential centres, the schemes for training and assessing Mountaineering Instructors have had to be expanded and revised.

The process of evolution in this still comparatively new field must continue. The implications and responsibilities, affecting as they do the whole concept and practice of education, must increasingly concern many others besides the Mountain Leadership Training Boards. Whatever developments may come about, however, those concerned with the training of the leaders must surely continue to regard their prime responsibility as ensuring that all those young people who are led on the mountains do so in the greatest possible safety, with enjoyment. That is what the scheme is all about and I hope that it remains so.

JOHN W. COOK, *Chairman,*
Scottish Mountain Leadership Training Board

Author's Note

These notes have been compiled to assist candidates for the Summer and Winter Mountain Leadership Certificates. It was never intended that they should compete with the many excellent books which already exist on the subject of mountaineering, but rather, that they should supplement these works, drawing attention to new material where appropriate and summarising the special requirements of the Certificate. For this reason certain chapters have been treated more fully than others, especially those which deal with subjects not covered by existing publications; for example, exposure and its relevance to expedition planning, snow structure and the development of avalanche hazard and so on. Other topics, such as rock climbing and snow and ice climbing, which have been exhaustively covered elsewhere are regarded more from the point of view of the instructor and the arrangement of subject matter than from any technical standpoint. This, inevitably, has led to a certain lack of continuity for which I must take full responsibility.

Finally, I should like to record my thanks to those members of the Board and others who have made individual contributions to the booklet and, in particular, to Ralph Blain, Murray Scott, Roger Mansfield, Barbara Spark and Hamish Brown, and to the staff at Glenmore Lodge.

Although the basic content of the scheme remains much the same, new, or extensively revised, material may be found under the following headings: route card, party leadership, danger, security on steep ground, weather, effects of heat, improvisation (for mountain rescue), select bibliography, first aid, belaying on snow and ice, snow shelters, snow blindness, the snow cover and avalanches, avalanche classification.

In this revised edition there are many new diagrams and many of the old ones have been redrawn. I should like to thank Brian Chambers for undertaking most of this work and Loch Eil Centre for affording him the time to do it.

ERIC LANGMUIR

Introduction

The element of risk is a fundamental theme running through all outdoor activities. In fact it is their mainspring. It is present even in the most controlled of conditions. It is present in the imagination of the novice rock climber – 'Will the rope really hold me if I fall?' Of course it will, but the doubt and fear are there and must be overcome. It is present too in the unexpected, in the objective dangers of our sport; the hold that weakens; the rock that falls; the lightning that strikes; and through the actions and mistakes of others. To avoid these multitudinous hazards we would do well to stay in our beds.

How then can we preserve some sort of balance between the adventurous element of outdoor activities on the one hand and the safety element on the other? At first sight the two appear to be incompatible and yet how often one finds that the top performer in a particular field is also the safest.

The answer seems to lie in the right sort of combination of training and experience. It matters not whether the training is given by more experienced friends or by an instructor at a mountain centre. The vital thing is that it should be based on the accepted code of technique and safety. Far from detracting from enjoyment, observance of this code broadens the safety margin and enables more ambitious projects to be enjoyed in safety. There is no such thing as a fully trained mountaineer and it would be a bold man and a foolish one who claimed that he had nothing more to learn.

Experience is the tough school of graduate training where the techniques learned in the shadow of a leader can be put to the test. This experience should, as far as possible, be matched to the appropriate stage of training achieved. It would be foolhardy in the extreme for example to attempt to lead a difficult ice climb on the basis of a knowledge of summer rock climbing in the Lake District. No amount of training or attendance at courses can compensate for a lack of this practical and individual experience. No amount of climbing as second on the rope is going to produce a good leader. Certainly, it will produce a good second or a good 'party' man, but the decisions that count are made in the van and the potential leader must find his own feet here, without the comforting knowledge that he has a long-stop, should things go wrong. A decision without the pressure of consequence is hardly a decision at all. The Mountain Leadership Training Board recognises this and insists that all candidates gain a minimum of genuine leading experience before coming for their final course of Assessment.

To say that in this way we can achieve a balance between 'challenge' and 'safety' is wishful thinking. The best we can hope for is an uneasy truce. It is foolish to expect a youngster to equate these two sensibly and it is in this department that he needs most guidance. It is hoped that the Mountain Leadership Certificate will make this informed guidance more readily available to the ever increasing number of young people going into the hills.

The Summer Certificate

1 Navigation

Good navigation is the fundamental theme of the Mountain Leadership Certificate, and thorough familiarity with the subject is expected at Assessment. Far too many accidents can be traced to an original error in route finding. It is not enough just to be able to follow a set course in fine weather at a low level. Absolute certainty in blind navigation in the most severe weather conditions is required and experience of these conditions is an essential part of training whether it is obtained at the course or at some other time and place.

The assessment itself will be based on the points listed in the Syllabus (see Appendix B) and will take place throughout the week, from written and oral examination to practical navigation on each day's journey and on the final expedition. The maps used will normally be from the 1″ or 2½″ O.S. Series and candidates are expected to use a Silva or similar type of compass. Heavy prismatics and '3d. bit' compasses are equally unacceptable.

No person is entirely safe in the mountains if he cannot use map and compass no matter how knowledgeable and experienced the leader. For reasons outside his control the members of the party can become separated and therefore it is important that each individual should be given sufficient basic instruction to enable him to find his way to safety. In the field of navigation then the party leader must be able to give such basic instruction. Training is arranged with this in mind and hints are given on methods of instruction and teaching aids.

The lesson plan which follows does not set out to explain map and compass work but rather to act as a guide to both the student and to the potential instructor as to what should be covered and how. One thing is certain and that is that if properly put across it can be a fascinating and rewarding subject.

Lesson plan

Introduction

Topic	Content	Aids to Instruction
HISTORY OF NAVIGATION	Natural navigation of the ancient peoples of the world (e.g. Polynesians) and in primitive societies today. Stress 'home on base' reference system and paramount importance of OBSERVATION – No Sixth Sense! Map and Compass does not dispense with need for observation.	To stress need for training and discipline, blindfold and ask to walk to fixed point.
EARLY PICTORIAL MAPS	Describe some of the great exploratory journeys and show the maps resulting from them. Point out differences in methods of presentation.	Many fascinating old maps are now available as prints.
MODERN SURVEY METHODS	History of the Ordnance Survey. Triangulation to aerial photography.	For interest only.

The Map

Topic	Content	Aids to Instruction
THE MODERN MAP	Firmly establish meaning of map as plan or aerial view. Align photo, model and map to establish relationship between them.	Air photograph, relief model and map of the same area and on the same scale.
SCALE	Necessity for and selection of suitable scales for different purposes (e.g. motoring, cycling, walking, building). The representative fraction and continental scales ($2\frac{1}{2}''$ map equivalent to 1/25,000).	A series of maps of varying scales showing some easily recognisable feature, such as a loch, each with the area of the largest scale map marked in outline.
MAP REFERENCES	The grid system, national and international.	Best explained on a blackboard at first. Plenty of practice later both ways, map to reference and vice versa. Emphasise that a six-figure reference does not refer to a point, but to an area of 100 metres square.
CONVENTIONAL SIGNS	A shorthand system. Illustrate different methods of representation (pictorial, initials, colour etc.).	Various guessing games can be devised to stimulate interest. 'MAPPO', using map symbols instead of numbers, as in Bingo, is a useful game.
PLACE NAMES	Compare the common ones from Scotland, England, Wales and Ireland.	Always try to create an interest in the meaning of the Gaelic place names.

A practical session at this point, before the introduction of contours, breaks up the theoretical instruction and helps to consolidate what has been learned. Courses should be short and simple, following roads and tracks and students should be accompanied, at least initially, so that their problems can be sorted out before they lose the thread.

Contours

CONTOUR LINES	Trace the history of the representation of relief on old maps. Firmly establish the principle of contour lines and the vertical interval between them. This is a crucial point in the understanding of maps. Use every aid at your disposal.	Plumpudding maps, hatchuring, colouring etc. Show examples. ■ Stone in trough. Add water inch by inch and mark water line on stone. ■ Slice up half a turnip or potato. ■ Use a stack of glass trays, each with a single contour line drawn on it superimposed on the original map. ■ A relief model before plastering showing stepped structure. ■ Sand tray work.
	Gradients, convex and concave slope, spurs, valleys and other topographical features.	Illustrate with examples from prepared map and also by use of models as above.

A practical session should follow bringing in various aspects of relief. The terrain must be suitably chosen so that the differences of relief are sufficiently clear on the map.

The Compass

Topic	Content	Aids to Instruction
ORIGINS	The magic needle of the Chinese. Where it points and why. Eight points of the compass – degrees – angles (Bearings).	Charts and blackboard.
NORTH POINTS	Magnetic and Grid or True North.	At the elementary stage do not confuse the issue by distinguishing between Grid North and True North. Use a world globe.
THE COMPASS	The Silva Compass and its component parts. Explanation of its use as:	Large plastic model available from B. J. Ward.
	■ a protractor, e.g. measuring angles (bearings) on the map.	Warn of effect of metal objects such as cameras, ice axes, etc.
	■ a compass, e.g. (i) Setting the map; (ii) Taking a bearing out of doors on a feature and the identification of this on the map. This involves the conversion of a magnetic to a true bearing and the use of the compass again as a protractor.	Plenty of examples until familiar.
	As in (i) measuring a bearing on the map, converting it to a magnetic bearing and setting this on the compass.	More examples. Insist on a rough visual check of the angle from the map.
WALKING ON A BEARING	Matching-up needle and walking on bearing set. Hints for use in bad conditions.	Practise exhaustively later.
TIME AND DISTANCE	Speed in relation to terrain and other factors. Naismith's rule as a rough guide (3 m.p.h. + $\frac{1}{2}$ hour per 1000 ft. climbing).	Adjust for conditions underfoot and overhead, load carried and fitness, see p. 36.
ROUTE SELECTION	Choice of best route. Essential bearings, escape routes, etc. Route card with estimated times. Safety precautions and methods in bad visibility.	Fill in sample route cards for various expeditions.
ON THE MARCH	Compensation for detours. Encourage use of natural advantages of terrain and deliberate 'AIM-OFF' to hit target. Error alertness and early correction.	Practice using maps of different scales: 1:10,000 and 1:20,000. These are standard scales for orienteering.
RESECTION	Establish location with bearings to visible features.	When using the Silva system there is no need to convert these bearings to back bearings when plotting them on the map.

Much of this instruction is best done out of doors. If at all possible each phase of theoretical instruction should be immediately followed by practical work to implant it firmly in the mind of the student.

Simple navigation courses can be great fun if intelligently laid out. They should if possible encircle the base so that a bad mistake can always be rectified by a quick return for further instructions. The course should not be too long and should become progressively more difficult towards the finish. In safe country students should travel singly or in pairs. In larger groups all the calculations tend to be done by the brightest ones. Problems of all kinds may be set en route including identification of features, sketch notes, collection of rock or plant specimens and so on; anything in fact which will stimulate the student to practice the skills previously learned indoors. The sport of Orienteering and simple map-making by compass traverse are other excellent ways of encouraging an interest in Navigation.

Finally it is well to remember that this skill is really only put to the test in a situation of stress and anxiety when perhaps conditions have deteriorated to such an extent that visibility is reduced almost to nil. It is under this sort of pressure that you cannot afford to make a mistake.

Metric Conversion of Naismith's Rule

This simplifies to five kilometres per hour plus half an hour for every three hundred metres of climbing. The small increase in speed is compensated by a slightly smaller height factor.

In estimating the time to be allowed for groups of youngsters it is best to use a modification of Naismith's Rule, namely: Two and a half miles per hour plus one hour for every fifteen hundred feet of climbing. Converted into metric units this closely approximates to:

Four kilometres per hour plus one hour for every four hundred and fifty metres of climbing.

2   Hillwalking

Number in party

Without a doubt this is the most important and yet the most neglected of all the factors concerned with mountain safety. Perhaps this is because it can never be formulated as an unvarying rule. There are too many other factors which have a bearing on the number of people who can safely be taken on a mountain walk: the length of the route, the type of ground surface and special difficulties of the terrain such as rock ridges and so on, the conditions to be expected overhead and underfoot, for example, wind, rain and snow and the fitness, age and sex of the members of the party. Not only are large parties of 15, 20 and sometimes even 30 highly dangerous on the hill, but they stifle interest and make good instruction impossible.

One person cannot possibly look after such large groups even in the easiest of terrain and when things go wrong troubles tend to multiply in proportion to the number of people in the party.

As a general rule hillwalking groups should number between three and ten, the ideal being about six; the sort of number the leader can be aware of without actually counting heads. If the route is a long one or perhaps one which involves some scrambling or ridge walking, six should be taken as the maximum. Three is taken to be the minimum safe number since in the event of an accident one member of the party can stay with the injured person while the other goes to summon help. This minimum becomes the maximum if long sections of difficult ground are to be encountered; the sort of ground which necessitates the use of a safety rope and demands of the leader a basic knowledge of rock climbing and rope handling.

The leader should never allow those in his care to go off alone in potentially dangerous country. This should not be taken to mean that a group must always be accompanied by a 'qualified' person. Programmes should be planned to encourage initiative and independence, but within a carefully chosen framework, which is judged by the leader to be well within the capabilities and experience of the group. For example, at an appropriate stage in their training, it may be more profitable for a party of young mountaineers to plan and execute a journey on their own through easy hill country, than to follow a more difficult route in the wake of an experienced leader. There is a time and a place for both in the scheme of things, but the opportunities which exist in the more gentle hills, usually closer to home, should not be ignored.

Equipment and clothing

The equipment carried by each member of the party must be checked by the leader before leaving base. A full list of equipment is given in Appendix E.

■ Each member of the group should have:
Map / compass / whistle / rucksack / large polythene bag / personal first aid kit / lunch / emergency ration, and in winter: Ice axe / torch / goggles in addition to the clothing and spare items mentioned below.

■ The party leader should have in addition:
120 feet of 9 mm Rope / a comprehensive first aid kit / duvet jacket or sleeping bag / mini flare pack or red flare.

As with personal equipment, clothing must be checked before departure. Boots should be comfortable and allow for one pair of thick stockings. Blisters must be treated immediately and not allowed to develop into deep sores. Woollen underwear is recommended for winter wear though string vests are popular as the wide mesh retains body heat and helps to prevent the top clothing becoming wet with perspiration.

Breeches or trousers, but not jeans, should be worn. Remember that several thin sweaters afford greater warmth and flexibility than one thick one. For all high level walking a waterproof anorak or cagoule is essential. Intelligent use of clothing can greatly increase the comfort of the walk. Don't let your party labour uphill wearing all their clothing. If practicable insist that they remove the outer layers and put them on again during rest periods. Spare clothing, including sweater, gloves, stockings, and over-trousers should be wrapped in a polythene bag and carried in the communal sack. A balaclava helmet and gloves should be taken on all expeditions when cold conditions are likely to be encountered.

Method

■ On roads or flat ground journeys are usually measured by miles, but on the hills it is more expedient to measure in hours. A rough guide when estimating the time of a walk for an average lightly equipped party is to allow one hour for every three miles plus half an hour for each thousand feet of climbing.

Route cards giving estimated times of arrival at various points, together with compass bearings, are invaluable in poor conditions. Escape routes should be noted and a bad weather alternative entered on the card. A sample route card is shown in figure 1.

■ Speed is of less importance than economy of effort. To hurry, except in extenuating circumstances, is foolish.

'Tail end Charlies' must be encouraged and not left to struggle on their own to become exhausted and depressed. Keep together and on no account send any member of the party back on his own. Except in dire emergency the party should act as a single unit.

■ There is no set *best position* for the leader of a party. He may be at the front, at the back, or in the middle. The position he adopts will depend on the circumstances prevailing at the time. Normally, of course, he will be in front, having appointed the next most experienced member of the party to bring up the rear.

■ Rhythm is essential to good hill walking: jerky movements, springing and flexing the knees by taking too high a step tire the muscles and should be avoided. The leg should be allowed to swing forward like a pendulum; the natural swing of the body assists this movement.

ROUTE CARD

*Objective:*_____ *Date:*_____

Location	Grid Reference	Magnetic Bearing	Distance	Height		Description of ground	Time
				Gained	*Lost*		
		←————————————— *Starting Position*					
Total							
Add ten minutes per hour							

Time Out: _____ *Time Back:* _____

It is dark at: _____

ESCAPE ROUTES		
1.	2.	3.

Fig. 1: Sample Route Card

NAMES OF PARTY		EQUIPMENT IN PARTY		
LEADER		*IN SUMMER*		
		Anorak	*Map*	*Whistle*
ASSISTANT		*Boots*	*Compass*	*Rations*
		Safety Rope	*Watch*	*First Aid*
		Survival Bag/ Tent	*Flares*	
		EXTRA IN WINTER CONDITIONS		
		Ice Axe	*Crampons*	*Torch*
		Balaclava	*Over-Trousers*	*Sleeping-Bag/ Duvet*
		Gloves/Mitts	*Goggles*	*Gaiters*

WEATHER FORECAST				
WIND				
Speed/Force		*Becoming*		
Estimated at Altitude		*Becoming*		
Direction		*Becoming*		
TEMPERATURE				
Sea Level		*Becoming*		
Estimated at Altitude		*Becoming*		
Cloud Base		*Becoming*		
Freezing Level		*Becoming*		
Outlook:				

Fig. 1: Sample Route Card, reverse side

There should be no conscious use of the leg muscles. To assist rhythm and balance the hands should be kept free at all times. Spare clothes, etc., should be carried in the rucksack or tied round the waist.

To maintain rhythm, the same speed of pace should be used on all types of ground, the length of the pace being shortened for steep or difficult ground and lengthened for easy ground.

■ The feet should be placed down flat with a deliberate step, resting the heels on any available projections such as stones or tufts of grass. Where the slope is very steep, zig-zagging will assist the walker. Good rhythm and setting the feet is the sign of the experienced hill walker.

■ When descending, overstriding and putting the foot down heavily should be avoided as these jar the body and therefore fatigue the walker. A controlled descent can be assisted by placing the toes against projections. Running downhill, though good fun, can be tiring. A good walker uses downhill periods to rest the muscles.

Scree running is also fun, but it is bad for boots and unless closely supervised can be dangerous. If you have to negotiate a scree make absolutely sure that your party is deployed in such a way that stones dislodged by one do not fall onto another.

■ Constant stopping and starting breaks up walking rhythm and should be avoided. Halts should only be made at fixed intervals based on time and ground; these halts should be of a short duration, on average 5 – 10 minutes every hour. Large meals should be avoided – 'a little and often' being the better approach to eating during a day on the hills. It is a good plan to retain a portion of the day's food until all difficult ground has been crossed and so maintain a reserve of food in case the unforeseen should occur.

Most streams in the mountains are fit to drink from. The body needs to replace fluid lost in sweat, in breathing, etc., and contrary to popular belief drinking is to be encouraged – 'little and often' once again being the safest maxim.

■ Constant vigilance should be exercised, as weather conditions can deteriorate with extreme rapidity in hill country. Check the weather forecast before leaving.

Changes of weather can produce serious problems for a walker, and great care should be taken that one does not over-reach one's ability. Most accidents due to weather occur through rashness. Act before the weather dictates its own terms.

■ Exposure is an ever present danger with young people in the mountains and all leaders must be familiar with its recognition and treatment. If your party is fit, dry, well fed and watered and in good spirit you have little to fear. If they are not, then you must modify your route to suit their condition and capabilities. 'It is the additional factor of physical exhaustion over and above cold which kills quickly. Death has overtaken whole parties who, thinking they must keep moving at all costs, have bashed on, instead of resting in some shelter before exhaustion supervened.' *Dr. Duff.*

■ No attempt must be made to cross mountain streams in spate where there is possible danger to life unless each member of the party can be adequately safeguarded. Youngsters should not be given routes to follow independently which might involve the crossing of such streams.

■ Severe electrical storms are unusual in British mountains. In the event of one, do not seek shelter under overhangs or in cracks in the cliff face or against large prominent boulders. Avoid being the prominent object in the neighbourhood. Get off peaks and ridges and sit it out on open coarse-blocked scree. There is no need to throw away your axe, camera or other ironmongery – you may need them later and they do not 'attract' lightning any more than you do yourself.

■ Rope the party together when visibility is very poor and when there is the likelihood that a slip might develop into a dangerous slide. Remember too that a small error in navigation can lead you to the edge of a cliff.

■ In addition to its chilling effect the wind can exert sufficient force to sweep a party off its feet. Be particularly careful round the tops of corries or on exposed ridges where a fall could be disastrous.

■ Good technique and safety measures can be learned. Good leadership and instruction is an art which embraces more than mere technical skill. Your job as a leader of a party is to stimulate interest and safe enjoyment in everything which the mountains have to offer.

Danger

It must be stated again that danger, or some element of it, is present in almost every mountain situation and varies infinitely in quantity and quality. Obviously, some attempt at assessment can be made, but this is compounded by the interaction of human factors. This is one area where knowledge of individual behaviour is of vital importance. Danger can be separated into two components – subjective and objective. Over the latter we have no control. The risk is inherent in the situation. The more ambitious the undertaking, the greater the degree of exposure to objective danger. It is clear, therefore, that this aspect of danger should be at a minimum during the novitiate period and reach a peak later on. However, it is important to acknowledge that some degree of real risk is always present.

Subjective danger, on the other hand, is that element of risk which comes under the control of the individual. It is modified by a number of factors, the most significant of which is experience. In the early stages there is a relatively high degree of risk. Accident records show that this is a vulnerable phase of an individual's experience and there is obviously a great deal to be said for competent guidance at this time. The level of subjective risk is reduced as the novice gains more experience.

The novice is certainly exposed to a high level of subjective danger. To a certain extent, this is offset by a lesser exposure to objective danger. The total situation can be immeasurably improved by competent leadership, since it is largely the leader's experience which provides the measure of subjective danger to a party. It would also appear that continued participation at an ever increasing level of difficulty involves a fairly steady increase in the overall level of risk. This will reach a peak and then gradually fall away with advancing years and the decline in the level of participation.

Leadership

Leading a successful walk with children calls for a great deal of skill. Walking holds none of the immediate thrills and feeling of adventure inherent in rock climbing or skiing. In fact, children often find walking boring and it is the job of the leader to counteract this by every possible means. He may do this through his choice of terrain, which in itself may create interest, or he may do it by observation and discussion of particular aspects of the environment. Or again, he may do it simply through his ability to find a common bond with the children and stimulate their interest.

The aim and purpose of each day's activity should be clear in the mind of the leader. However, it should always be possible to alter this aim should the weather prove to be unsuitable for the activity planned. The leader must know what is justifiable in a given set of circumstances and be sufficiently imaginative and flexible to alter his plans should this be necessary. He should be careful not to confuse his own desires and ambitions with what is a suitable undertaking for the whole party.

It cannot be too strongly stated that leadership demands more than just the mere acquisition of knowledge and expertise, though these attributes are a very necessary part of the leader's make-up. In addition, he must:

■ be able to distinguish between difficulty and danger and, as suggested in the previous paragraph, be able to make a realistic assessment of the latter, whether its nature be objective or subjective.

■ be aware of the strengths and weaknesses of the party and know how to get the best out of each individual.

■ be able to see situations through the eyes and senses of his charges and to put their needs before his own.

■ be able to maintain good morale, especially in the face of difficulties and to make a detached judgement when danger threatens.

■ be a good manager, able to plan and to look after his party off the mountain as well as on it.

■ be flexible in action, ready to adapt and adjust and, indeed, to turn back, as circumstances dictate. *He must not be bound by a set of preconceived recipes* (usually obtained from a book such as this). No two situations are ever exactly alike and to apply a fixed formula invites disaster.

In the expression of all these qualities and many more unlisted, there is still room for the personal flair; the individual's own way of doing things. Indeed, many of the finest qualities of leadership are innate and cannot be acquired, either by reading, or by any form of training. However, the objective remains the same. The inspiration of a sense of trust, of confidence and the will to co-operate with other members of the group to achieve the goal, whether it be the attainment of a summit, or the safe return after a difficult retreat. It would be a remarkable person who possessed all of these qualities in full measure. It is in the widening of his experience that the aspirant will develop the qualities which, in turn, will help to make him a mature and responsible leader.

3 Camping and Expeditions

These notes deal with a vital part of the certificate work as much of young people's outdoor activity is based on camping and expeditions, which are influenced themselves by other factors (i.e. strength of party, weather). Misadventure could have serious consequences and candidates are urged to attain as much experience as possible.

Camping is the ability to live as comfortably as possible under any weather conditions in remote areas with the minimum of equipment needed to ensure adequate shelter, feeding, and expedition activity.

Leaders should constantly be teaching by example. Comfort, safety and enjoyment lie in a thousand little knacks, too numerous to list. These notes indicate some of the more important points. Many aspects of camping and expedition activity can be rehearsed beforehand, and this is essential, both for personal assurance and the safety of young people who cannot be watched all the time. The year of experience between Basic Training and Assessment is the time to acquire camping and expedition skills and routine.

The Party should be reasonably fit before starting. Care should be taken not to overburden. Check for anyone with disabilities or special medical requirements. Ensure parents signed approval to partake at their responsibility. Check insurance. If travelling, use 'Kwells'.

The Timetable should be flexible and there should be some progression from easy to more difficult undertakings. If the weather is severe, stay put if possible; certainly not moving merely to stick to an armchair plan. Mountain weather is unpredictable. Allow for this when planning. Do not attempt too long marches. Very hot weather can also be exhausting: if necessary be up at five and finish the day's walk by noon. Use local knowledge as well as maps, guides, etc.

Daily Routine An early start always pays off. Work out a system that can be used by the party each day. Everyone should be employed. From waking to departure should not be longer than two hours for an efficient team. Try to be settled in a new site before evening. Tents should, as far as possible, operate as independent units, though, if weather is set fair, it may be quicker for each tent to deal with one part of a meal. Two tents, pitched door to door, can also operate as a unit. Do not hesitate to stop for a 'brew-up' or a swim during the day. They are valuable mentally and physically. Check at the end of a trip to see what was carried and never used – question whether to take it again. Ensure that people wash adequately and change clothes before sleeping.

Food Adequate (some 4000 kilocalories per day) and appetising feeding is a vital part of any well run expedition. See to it that your party takes a hot breakfast and evening meal each day. A communal brew of hot, sweet tea immediately on arrival at the camp site is an excellent morale booster and paves the way to a good meal. Lightweight expeditions can make use of the wide range of dehydrated foods now available on the market. Be careful to select those which have a reasonably short cooking time and which can be cooked in a single pot. Dehydrated foods are of course expensive, but allow a great saving in weight and therefore of energy.

Personal Clothing A comprehensive list of recommended clothing and equipment is given in Appendix 'E'.

■ Never assume that the members of your party are properly kitted out. Before leaving inspect all equipment and personal clothing.

■ Insist on warm trousers or breeches and adequate head cover.

■ A waterproof outer is essential whether it be the specially designed cagoule or an ex W.D. gas cape. If of the latter type make sure that there is some means of tying it to the body in windy conditions.

■ All spare clothing must be carried in a polythene bag. Try to achieve a sensible balance between adequate protection and the extra weight to be carried.

■ A dry set of clothes should always be kept for night wear or emergency. Wet clothes can often be dried out over night and in any case it is normally better to put on damp clothes in the morning than risk wetting your dry change.

Boots and Care of Feet Boots are essential for comfort, safety and efficiency. Make sure they are broken in before an expedition and that they are kept clean and well maintained by replacement of the natural oils in the leather as necessary. They should offer good ankle support, they should protect the sole of the foot from sharp stones and they should be fairly rigid across the sole. Some flexibility in a forward direction makes for more comfortable walking and a bellows-type tongue helps to keep out the water. The limitations of the vibram or moulded rubber sole should be clearly understood. They are slippery on hard snow or ice, on vegetation of any kind and on wet, greasy rock.

The condition of your feet can make or mar an expedition. Keep them in good order and insist that your charges do the same: wash regularly / use clean, well fitting stockings or socks, a single pair of loop stitched stockings is best or two pairs of wool ones / toe nails should be cut straight and kept short / regular applications of surgical spirit harden the feet / the slightest irritation should be plastered at once.

Blisters are uncomfortable and a hindrance and potential danger to the whole party. They should be pricked with a sterilised needle to allow the liquid to escape and then plastered. Change the plaster daily and allow every opportunity for the area to harden up in the fresh air.

Load Packing and Carrying

TYPES

■ The framed sack of the 'Commando' style is quite unsuitable since it forces the wearer into a crouched position. However, better designs are available which are relatively light in weight, which distribute the load well and which allow ventilation of the back.

■ The pack frame can be adapted to carry a variety of loads and is generally accepted as being the most efficient method of carrying a heavy load.

■ The unframed sack is light and comfortable to carry and can be used as a mattress or to provide protection for the feet at night. There is no ventilation for the back and the weight tends to be rather more unevenly distributed.

PACKING

■ Articles needed during the journey or immediately on reaching the camp site should be on top or in side pockets, i.e. food for the day, first aid kit, tent and so on. / Do not have articles dangling from the outside of the sack. / Heavy articles should be kept as high as possible. / Balance the weight and avoid sharp edges and corners against the back. / Stove and fuel should be kept in a well sealed polythene bag and stored in a side pocket or well away from food. / Adjust shoulder and waist straps as necessary. All clothing and sleeping bag should be kept in polythene bags and the sack itself might benefit from a 500 gauge polythene bag liner.

WEIGHT

■ Your total load should never exceed one-third of the body weight and for young people 30 lbs. should be the absolute maximum.

CARRYING

■ As far as possible the load should be kept high on the back and in such a position that the weight acts vertically downwards through the spine. This principle has been used successfully for centuries by all the primitive people of the world.

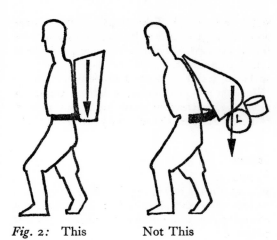

Fig. 2:   This   Not This

Tents

Poor quality tents should not be used in mountains. For the wet and windy conditions so common in the U.K. it is advisable to have a sewn-in ground sheet, down to earth all-round fly sheet and strong alloy 'A' poles front and rear. Many so called 'mountain tents' are in fact designed for high altitude work abroad in conditions of extreme dry-cold and are quite unsuited to our normal weather. Each tent should be a self-contained unit with its own stove, dixies, food, etc., sufficient for the occupants.

Siting the Camp

A good site should provide shelter from the prevailing wind. The ground should be as flat as possible and relatively free from lumps, tussocks and boulders. It should be well drained and safe from potential flooding. A handy water supply is almost essential though don't pitch too near a noisy mountain stream if you want an undisturbed night's rest. Trees may provide some protection from the wind but don't pitch directly underneath them; although they offer some immediate shelter from the rain eventually large drops form and these are much more effective in penetrating the fly sheet.

Tent Pitching

Even if the weather seems set fair allow for the worst when pitching your tent. Put the back end into the wind and peg out the groundsheet first to ensure tent shaping. Erect the windward end first and peg out all main guys. Other guys are pegged out in line with the tent seams. The valance may be weighted with stones, also the pegs, but do not place stones on top of guy lines. In a wind the sawing action frays them through in no time. There should be no wrinkles in the canvas and any unnatural strains should be corrected by adjusting guys. Door tabs should be tied in bows not knots.

Striking Camp

As far as the tents are concerned this is largely a matter of reversing the procedure for pitching. In bad weather it is usually possible to fold up the tent first under the protection of the fly sheet. All pegs should be cleaned and all the parts stowed away in their bags. On returning to base, tents should be hung to dry out thoroughly and examined carefully for any damage before storing. Check the site before leaving to see nothing is forgotten and no litter is left. After a few days it should be hard to tell that the site has been used.

Bedding – Warmth and Comfort

■ A sleeping bag is far lighter and warmer than blankets. It is worth buying a good quality down bag as it will last a long time with care. It should be kept dry and clean and stored unrolled.

■ Much cold comes from below and insulation is recommended. A sewn-in groundsheet helps. A layer or two of newspapers, tarred paper or frameless rucksack is useful. An air bed or foam mattress gives comfort as well as insulation.

■ In winter a second sleeping bag may be needed. Always do something about cold, if necessary light a stove or exercise, don't just lie!

■ It is often possible to pack the underside of the groundsheet with bracken, heather or grass to improve comfort and insulation.

■ It is more comfortable to sleep head uphill if on a slope.

■ Polythene bags are useful for storing: unwanted clothes (useful as pillow) / wet clothes if inside at all / personal belongings / sugar, salt, potato powder or anything else in breakable packets / emergency bags for travel sickness.

■ Boots should not be worn inside tents. Wet clothes should be taken off before entry if possible. If soaked to the skin, remove all clothing, get into sleeping bag and prepare hot, sweet drinks.

■ Store tins, wet clothes, ropes, anything sheep, cows, dogs will not eat, under the flysheets. Pans, stoves, water carriers should be easily within reach.

■ Tents without flysheets will leak if the canvas is rubbed. The obvious solution is a flysheet, otherwise movement has to be restricted. A small sponge is useful to mop up leak spots or spilt tea, etc.

■ Newspapers are useful in camping: for insulation under bedding / for cleaning material / to keep under supplies, cutlery or pans to prevent dirt or grease spreading / under a pullover for body insulation / helping to dry boots / helping to start fires.

■ The following are some useful items: Torch (remove battery to avoid accidental switch-on in travel); compass (Silva type are the 'best buy'); whistle (a pea whistle is better than a policeman's); maps (1″ O.S. are best); plastic paraffin jars; tin opener (small ones, costing 5p., can fold into a wallet); brillo pads; toilet paper; knife; spare bootlaces (for any purpose); first aid kit; a 120 ft. nylon 9 mm rope; emergency rations in a special box; cutlery; deep plate and mug (not china); plimsolls (wear on bare feet if wet, avoiding wet socks); a band saw can cut firewood easily; a small size fish slice is valuable; as is an egg whisk for mixing milk powder; sewing kit; shoe kit; writing materials; transistor (for weather forecasts); anti-midge cream and / or spray (May to October); alarm clock (folding); camera; small binoculars.

Hygiene

■ Water should be collected above the site and washing should be done below.

■ Nails should be clean and washing of hands insisted on after using lavatories or before handling food.

■ If at all possible take your rubbish home with you especially if the site is accessible and likely to be used frequently. Otherwise rubbish should be burnt and buried in a deep pit. Tins should be opened at both ends, flattened and burnt.

■ Glass is unnecessary in the first place (use plastic bags or containers or light tins and transfer jar contents into these) but on no account must be smashed. Take empties home! Livestock damage is caused by tins and glass carelessly disposed. Polythene bags are particularly lethal to animals.

■ Toilet facilities depend on length of stay. Where at all permanent, a latrine trench is advisable. Excrement must be buried at least 6″ below surface. There should be no trace left.

Stoves

TYPES

■ Gas: This is clean, requires no priming, but is expensive and, for half an hour before a cartridge runs out, burns at an infuriatingly low pressure.

■ Pressure stove: These require priming with solid 'Meta' fuel or meths, but give a wide variety of pressure. They are very cheap to run. Petrol stoves are not recommended for inexperienced young people.

SAFETY FACTORS

■ Changing Gas cartridges or filling stoves should be done in the open and away from candles or any naked light.

■ Experience in using stoves must be had before going off on expeditions when their lighting and use may have to be within tents or shelter.

■ As with all stoves, there is considerable danger of setting the tent alight when cooking is done inside the tent. If cooking outside is not possible because of weather conditions, adequate ventilation must be ensured. In addition to burning up Oxygen, combustion produces Carbon monoxide gas which may be highly dangerous in a sealed atmosphere.

■ Gas is heavier than air. During sleep, gas from leaking appliances could accumulate in a layer on the groundsheet (particularly if sewn in). Quite apart from the obvious danger of explosion, this layer could rise to nose level, with fatal results. *Store gas stoves and cylinders outside.*

■ Paraffin pressure stoves in fact burn paraffin vapour and pumping too soon will result in flooding. This causes dangerous flaring and soot is deposited which will ultimately choke the nipple. Pricking (only when needed) to clear stoves, as well as priming, should be done outside, if possible.

■ Make sure you have the correct fuel. Because

of this danger, parties of young people are advised to use paraffin stoves only. Petrol stoves always have additional risks.

■ Do not overfill a stove. When doing anything to a stove, always remove pans. When stirring pans, always hold on to the handle. Scalding accidents are common. Make sure handles are up or extended properly so that they do not hang down near the flame to become dangerously hot.

■ Patience is the most important point in stove control.

Fire in Tents

The main causes are: mis-use of stoves / cigarettes / candle or lighting.

PRECAUTIONS

See above, but also, do not fall asleep smoking or with a candle or stove left burning. (Elementary – but it happens constantly!) Long candles should be snapped in half to make them less unstable. Even placing them up on a tin usually ensures that if they topple they land end on and so extinguish the flame. Some safety holder is easily created. With other forms of lighting – wick or pressure lamps, etc., care must be taken to ensure adequate ventilation.

A small internal fire can quickly be smothered with a sleeping bag, with little damage to the bag but, if the roof or walls go up, it is vital to get out fast. Poles and, if necessary, main guys, should be collapsed to smother the fire. Any other method is ineffective as it is too slow. Exterior poles are useful for this. A stove giving real trouble should be thrown outside at once. Work stoves near the entrance – if you must have them inside at all.

Outdoor fires may be pleasant but great care must be taken to ensure no fire risk to tents and to forests or dry hillsides from falling hot sparks. Turf must be removed and replaced over the dead ashes. On no account should a smouldering fire be left. Rubbish can be burnt sometimes on the rocks of a river bed.

Failure of preparation and ineffective leadership in camping and expeditions can lead to: failure of achievement / dangerous situations or accidents / discomfort / discouragement.

4 Security on steep ground

It must be the first of priority the leader in the hills to avoid having to use the rope. If the ground is too steep or dangerous for the group, a retreat should be made, or an easier alternative found. Never-the-less, situations can, and do, arise when the use of the rope is necessary to safeguard the party.

The small amount of rock climbing included in the course is not intended to train leaders as rock climbers. Its purpose is to familiarise candidates with elementary techniques, to enable them to appreciate the limits of what should be attempted by a party without rock climbing experience, to recognise difficulties and potential dangers of terrain and to give competent help in cases of emergency. *Any safe method of rope management will be acceptable on assessment, but whatever method is used, it should involve the use of the rope alone.* It is emphasised that the techniques advocated here are not necessarily those which would be suitable for rock climbing. However, taken together, they provide a simple and safe method which can be followed by the non-climber and are applicable to almost any situation in which he is likely to find himself.

Assessment

The object of assessment is to discover whether or not the candidate is confident and familiar with the rope and that he can achieve speed of action in getting it into use.

He must:

■ be able to lead on easy ungraded rock on descent as well as ascent,

■ be able to find and use suitable anchors quickly,

■ be able to abseil,

■ be able to hold a falling second,

■ know the standard calls and signals used for communication,

■ be able to pass on simple instructions in all of these things,

■ be able to select a safe line up a rocky hillside and to know when to put on the rope.

The importance of the inclusion of this small amount of rock climbing in the syllabus as a means of understanding the proper use of a safety rope, cannot be overstressed. A rope is a vital piece of equipment for a mountain leader. Candidates must be aware of this emphasis and of the large gap which exists in their safe supervision of a party on the mountains, if they are not confident in their ability to cope with a situation requiring the use of a safety rope. There is no attempt to make them rock climbers in the normally accepted definition of the term.

It is worth remembering that there are many situations apart from graded rock climbs, when the rope is at least desirable and sometimes, essential, e.g.

■ a particularly nervous person, in an intimidating situation, may welcome a safety rope.

■ a person suffering from a minor injury (sprained ankle) may need the security of the rope.

■ used as a hand line.

■ crossing a gully, checking a line of descent, moving across frozen grass or old snow (Spring or Autumn hazard).

■ going to someone's assistance.

■ in an emergency when it may be necessary to extricate the party from an exposed situation, either up or down.

Leaders should always appreciate the technical difficulties as they appear to the novice and be sympathetic towards their mental condition under stress. Psychological and physical succour, brought about by the timely and proper use of the rope, can make the difference between a serious situation and safe leadership.

Any mountain leader ought to be in a position to advise young people in his care on all aspects of mountain safety, including differentiating between scrambling and rock climbing and in recognisin potentially dangerous terrain, where a rope may have to be used to safeguard the party.

Instruction

To teach the rudiments of the skills of movement on rock, to give satisfactory guidance in the selection of sound belays, to make the candidate confident as an abseiler and to allow him an opportunity to lead, means that a full day's instruction is necessary. Since it is unreasonable to expect the mountain walker to equip himself with the impedimenta of the rock climber (slings, karabiners, etc.), the instruction should be given with the equipment which is normally carried by the party leader on a mountain walk, i.e. the rope. It is recommended that the safety rope should be at least 9 mm diameter nylon and a minimum length of 120 feet. Experience of handling, and holding a fall, on this size of rope, is essential. Rope which is any thinner than this makes both holding and abseiling difficult, as well as painful.

As a standard approach is considered desirable, and to emphasise the need for planned instruction, a lesson plan is given below. Progress will depend on the students themselves and the staff available, but all the topics listed must be covered in basic training. The method advocated is the simplest one which can be applied safely to most situations which are likely to arise.

Lesson Plan

Topic	Content	Notes
EQUIPMENT	Strength and properties of nylon ropes. Limitations in use. Handling properties of ropes of different diameters.	Indoor session. Recommended rope: 9 mm diameter, 120 ft. in length.
THE ROPE	Coiling, carrying, hanging, storing.	
TYING ON	Overhand, figure of eight, bowline. If there are more than 2 on the rope, the middle man (men) ties on with a figure of eight.	Compare effectiveness. Note how a mistake in tying a figure of eight results in an overhand knot; still a safe knot. Leave at least a 1 ft. tail, which may be tied off with an overhand knot.

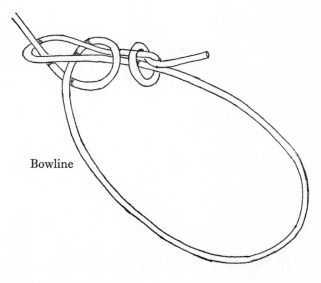

Overhand

Figure of Eight
NOTE: Instead of a stopper knot, the free end can be tucked through with the loop.

Bowline

3: Knots for tying on to the rope

Topic	Content	Notes
BELAYING	Anchor selection and testing.	Examine for cracks. Kick or shake. If possible the anchor point should be above waist height.
	Position of stance in relation to belay.	The climber takes up his belaying position so that the expected pull on the rope is, as far as possible, on the same line as the ropes leading from him to the anchor. The second man should be clearly visible.

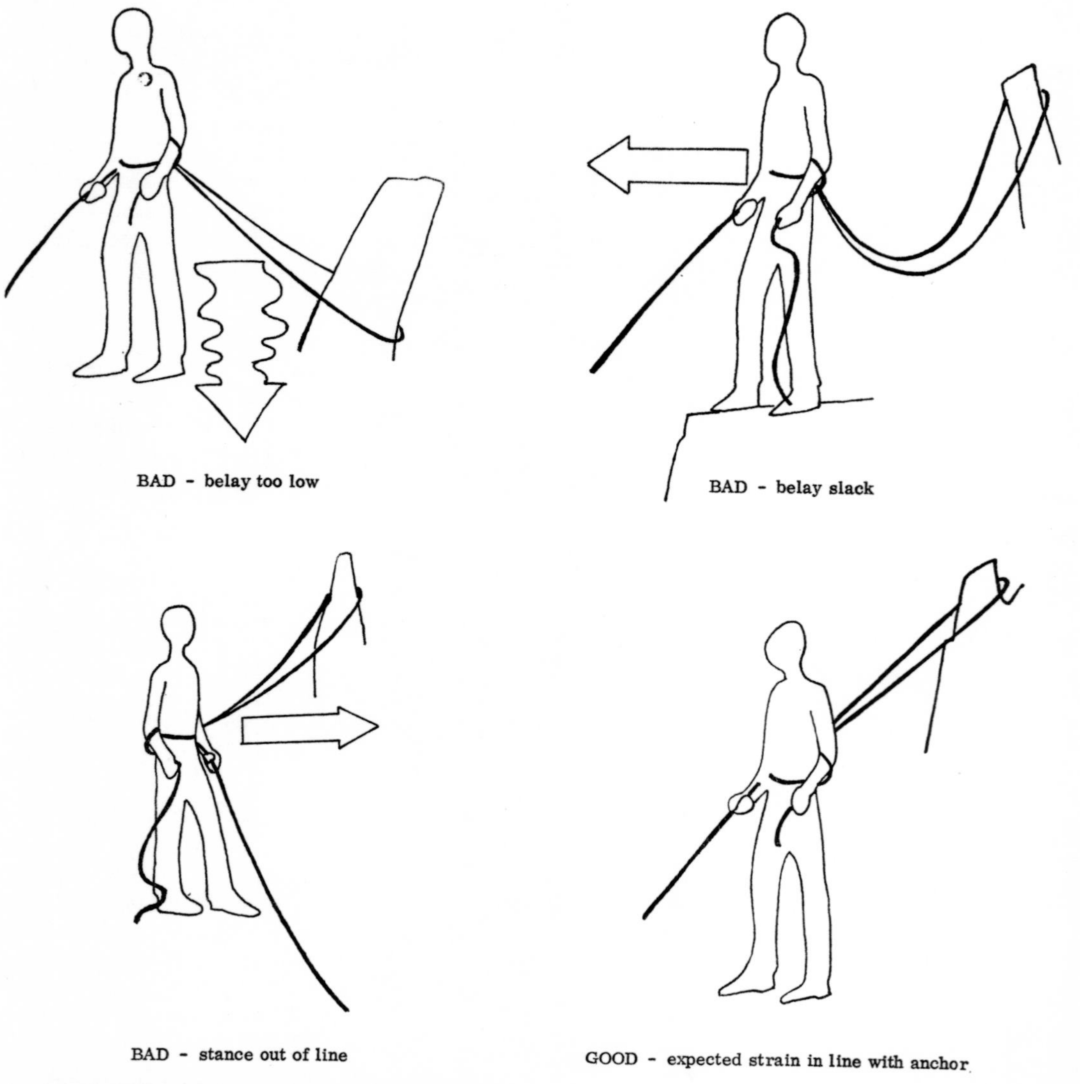

BAD - belay too low

BAD - belay slack

BAD - stance out of line

GOOD - expected strain in line with anchor

Fig. 4: Examples of good and bad positioning

Topic	Content	Notes

THE SPIKE BELAY   I. Tied off at waist.

The rope from the waist is placed round the spike. The climber takes up his stance.

A tuck is taken through the waist loop to about arms length and the loop so formed is used to tie off all three, or any two, ropes, with a figure of eight knot or 2 half hitches. The clothes should be lifted over the waist tie to protect it from friction heat. The slack rope is taken in, hand over hand and piled loosely at the feet until contact is established with the second. The active rope is then passed over the head to the waist, where it is held in the hand, a twist being taken round the fore-arm on the side furthest away from the person climbing (the 'inactive' rope).

. 5: Belaying on rock. The spike belay

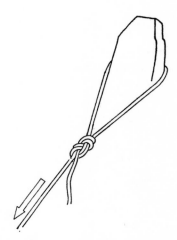

Fig. 6: The spike belay tied off at the anchor.

2. Tied off at the anchor.

An alternative method:
A figure of eight, or overhand knot, is tied in a bight of rope, of suitable length, taken from the waist. The loop formed is then placed over the anchor. This allows the leader to untie himself from the rope if necessary, while still leaving the second man secured to the belay.

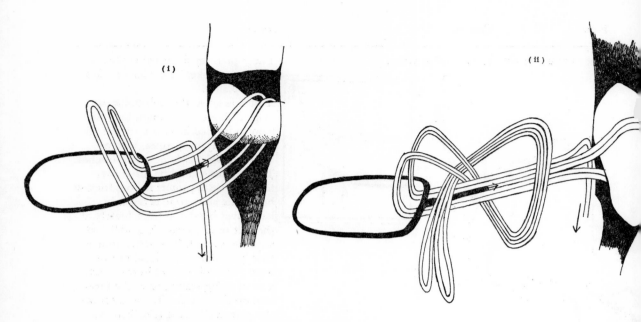

Fig. 7(a): Thread Belay with both loops tied together

Topic	Content	Notes
THE THREAD BELAY	1. Double figure of eight system.	In theory, the best type of belay since it resists a pull from any direction. It is tied in a similar way to the spike belay, except that a loop of rope is passed through the thread and back to the waist. Here, a tuck is taken through the waist tie, together with an equal loop from the active rope. The two loops (4 strands of rope) are then tied off round all the ropes from the waist, as in Figure 7(a).

Alternatively, the two loops may be tied off independently, as shown in Figure 7(b).

Disadvantages – it is a bulky knot and if the thread is far back from the stance, it uses up a lot of rope.

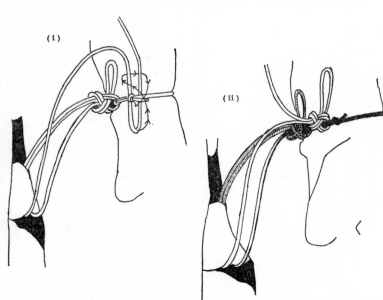

Fig. 7(b): Thread Belay with both loops tied off independently

Topic	Content	Notes
	2. By untying and passing the rope through the thread	An acceptable alternative, when operating from a SAFE position, is to untie and thread the end of the rope through the belay and tie on again. The active rope can then be taken through the waist tie and tied off as in the normal spike belay. This method is economical of rope but, of course, it may not always be possible to move freely about the stance unroped.
BRINGING UP THE SECOND MAN	Bring the rope over the head and around the waist. The rope is now going from one hand, around the waist and into the other hand. The inactive rope should have a turn round the arm in which it is held. The active leg should be advanced in line with the active rope. Gloves should be worn.	See Figure 8 below. When taking in never remove your hands from the rope. This is achieved by passing the rope from (A) to (B), (A) being the hand on the active side. I: (A) holds both ropes while (B) slides up to position II. II: (A) and (B) grip their own ropes, gloves should be worn, and the rope is pulled round the waist by an extension of arm (B) and a flexion of arm (A). III: (A) slides down to adopt Position I. Always keep a tight rope to the second man.

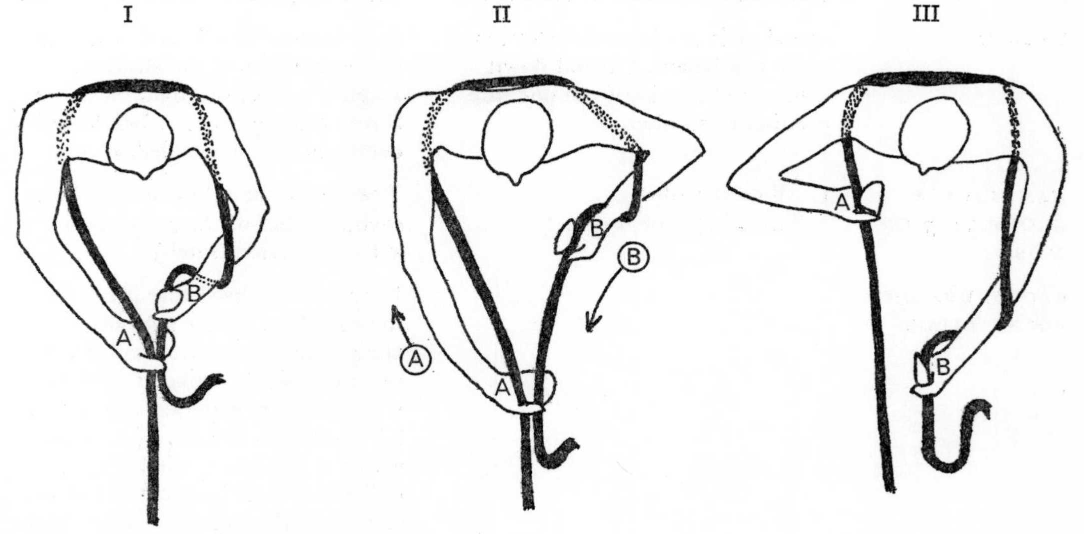

I   II   III

Fig. 8: Bringing up the second man

Topic	Content	Notes
COMMUNICATIONS	Taking in, *that's me*, climb when you're ready, *climbing*, OK. Other terms include 'slack' and 'take in'.	Importance of standardisation. Loud and clear use of these terms by everyone. Note, especially, that the second does not remove his belay until he has heard the call, 'climb when you're ready'.
SCRAMBLING	Over broken rock and boulders before reaching crag.	Observation of balance and movement. Warming up. Familiarity with adhesive properties of footwear.
LOOSE ROCK	Care in handling. Warning shout, 'Below'.	Safety of group.
SCREE	Ascent and descent. Scree running. Care necessary.	Positioning of party to avoid rock fall. Warning to avoid screes which cannot be seen in their entirety.
CLIMBING	Plenty of practice on descent. Use of feet, three point contact, selection of holds, soundness of rock.	Simple climbs with, perhaps, one more difficult one to aid differentiation. Avoid complex moves.
HOLDING A FALL	Second falls only. Use the recommended safety rope, 9 mm nylon.	The instructor should be close at hand. Check all belays. This is a controlled trial. Gloves should be worn.
ROUTE SELECTION	Choice of easiest line up rock buttress. Estimation of difficulties.	This may be practised at any suitable opportunity during the day.
LEADING	Speed or lack of speed. Selection of route and belays. Up and down. Concept of moving from one safe position to another.	Routes must be selected well within the capabilities of the student. Implications of diagonal movement. Stress consequences of bad leader decisions as to route, belays, etc.
HANDLING A GROUP OF 3 OR MORE	1. All on the rope. 2. Throwing rope down.	The leader should personally bring each member of the group over the difficult section (Pitch).
PROCEDURE ON A ROCKY RIDGE		It must be realised that it is impossible to secure a group completely on a narrow ridge with precipitous side walls. Only those with sufficient experience should be taken on such terrain. In an emergency and if in any doubt, each individual must be secured separately over the exposed section of the ridge.

Topic	Content	Notes
ABSEILING	Classic method. Selection of suitable anchor points above waist level. Abseil straight down and at an angle to R. and L. Stress that this is an emergency procedure for the leader. Give examples.	Always use a safety rope in training Students should do enough of this to feel that they could abseil happily. without it in an emergency. Use 9 mm rope, doubled, with a figure of eight knot, forming a loop in the middle, to go over the abseil point. Do not use the belay as the abseil point. Short abseils. Abseiling may be introduced whenever time and instructional staff will allow.

Fig. 9: Abseiling, using the 'classic' method

Topic	Content	Notes
MOVING TOGETHER	Not on rock.	This is an advanced technique which depends for its success on the absolute reliability of each member of the party. For this reason it should not be used by leaders, save as a means of keeping the party together in otherwise safe terrain. e.g. in bad visibility, or in a high wind.

Topic	*Content*	*Notes*
FIXED ROPE	Of limited use, usually in descent and certainly not in any situation where a slip could have serious consequences.	The rope should be tied with wrist loops (overhand) and then firmly secured at top and bottom and at any place where there is a change of direction.

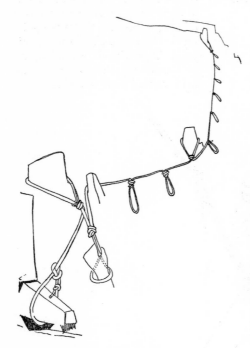

Fig. 10: Setting up a Fixed Rope

Further Training

It is emphasised again, that the techniques advocated for basic training in mountain leadership are not necessarily those which would be taught to rock climbers, particularly since no special equipment is used, other than the rope. However, the possibility of progression should always be borne in mind by the instructor and interested candidates may be taken a stage further.

Procedures on difficult terrain, such as a narrow ridge, deserve special consideration. It is the leader's responsibility to organise the necessary group practice before embarking on any more serious undertaking. In deciding the best and safest method of tackling a particular problem, he must take into account the terrain and the possible consequences of a slip, the time available and the prevailing conditions. He must so arrange matters that he is able to supervise and safeguard the less able in the group

Conclusion

The effectiveness of this instruction depends on:
■ Candidates understanding the reasoning behind the techniques.
■ An adequate number of competent instructors, who also understand the place of this subject in the syllabus and its treatment. The number of instructors ought to be in the ratio 1:4 for instruction and 1:2 for assessment.
■ The selection of a suitable piece of rocky terrain to illustrate all the main points mentioned.

During the course, instructors will teach the elements of party management in emergencies which require the use of a rope. They should explain who carries the rope and where, describing the ground on which a party might require more than one rope, and emphasising to leaders that it will ease their lot if the members of the party know how to use a rope before they go on the hill. It is far too late to begin instruction in rope handling when the crisis has developed. This means that the leader must be able to give basic instruction to his party. His ability to do so will be assessed.

Candidates are likely to be assessed on ground which will involve them in some decision-taking. This is often a source of difficulty and danger with inexperienced parties. When to put on the rope, what to do in an area of loose rock, how to select sound belays in the right position and so on. Training situations must, therefore, be made as realistic as possible.

Finally, it must be said again, that the first duty of the mountain leader is to avoid a situation where the use of the rope becomes necessary.

5 River Crossing

River crossing is an emergency procedure which should only be attempted when,
■ the water is clearly fordable.
■ any potential danger can be adequately safeguarded by the use of the rope.
■ the alternatives to crossing are more hazardous than the crossing itself.

Preparation

The aim of the training is twofold
■ To acquaint climbers with the dangers of streams in flood.
■ To suggest safe methods of crossing streams which are fordable.

Few climbers or walkers have any idea of the forces involved in moving water. 'I had no idea it was so powerful' is an often heard remark during training sessions on the river. It is one of the prime objects of training to provide this experience under controlled and supervised conditions. It has been said that it is impossible to control conditions and that for this reason river crossing should not be taught to mountain leaders. Burns and rivers are as much part of the mountain environment as rocks and learning the safest way to cross them is as important as learning to abseil. Like the latter it is not intended that the leader should pass on this skill to his own charges, but rather that, fully aware

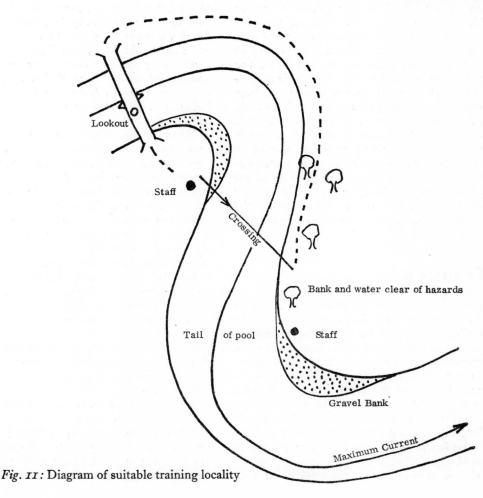

Lookout

Staff

Crossing

Bank and water clear of **hazards**

Staff

Tail of pool

Gravel Bank

Maximum Current

Fig. 11: Diagram of suitable training locality

of the dangers, he can make a valid decision to cross or not and that if he decides to cross then the crossing is made safely.

It is perfectly possible to select a safe and suitable section of the river at any time according to its condition. For training purposes several alternative sites should be chosen each with its own indicator to show when the water has reached its optimum height. If the river is too high at one crossing point perhaps a locality on a tributary would offer better conditions. Normally, difficulty is experienced in finding water of sufficient depth and pace. In this case the session should be postponed until conditions improve, since much of the point of the exercise will be lost if the crossing is too easy. Where possible the crossing should be made from shallow to deep and from slack to fast moving water with an easy avenue of return either across a bridge or by wide easy shallows. These conditions are commonly found at bends in the river where the form of the river carries the main current to the outside of the bend. The stretch chosen must be free of hazards such as submerged trees, dangerous undertows, high difficult banks and so on and the outflow should be into a quiet pool with a gravelly, shallow tail.

A member of staff should be stationed at this point in case a fielding operation should be necessary. A look-out should also be posted upstream of the crossing to give warning of the approach of any heavy floating debris. Life jackets should be worn by all those actually engaged in crossing the river whenever the rope is not in use.

Training

In mountain areas where there is quick run off of surface rain water into the burns even the smallest streams can become raging torrents in a matter of moments. In this condition they are potentially very dangerous and if there is any doubt at all about whether or not they can be crossed then either make a detour or stay put until the floods subside. This decision is the key to the whole problem. It can only be taken by the party leader on the spot, bearing in mind all the factors relevant to the safety of those in his charge.

If it is considered that the river is fordable,

then certain fundamental rules must be observed:

■ Inspect as much of the river as possible before selecting the best crossing point. It is often quite easy to ford a river near its mouth. Mountain burns running into lakes normally flatten out and consequently slow down in the last half mile or so. Generally, the water is quite deep but slow-flowing. Again, however, great care must be taken in crossing, particularly with the non-swimmer.

■ The area selected should be free of obstructions, submerged or otherwise, which could snag the ropes. Avoid high banks, and make sure that the exit point is reasonable, with good access along both banks. Inspect the outflow. As far as possible it should also meet the above conditions.

■ Small and/or light people will be swept off their feet at shallower depths. Make allowances for this when selecting the best crossing point.

■ Packs should be carried high on the back, making sure that any waist belt or head strap is undone for quick release if this should prove necessary. In really fast water, stones or other ballast can be added to the sack to increase stability.

■ Never remove boots even when fording a small burn. For comfort, stockings may be taken off and boots worn on bare feet. Trousers too may be removed to reduce friction.

■ Do not test the force of the water without being secured from the bank.

■ Do not attempt to cross by jumping from boulder to boulder where one slip, so easily done, could result in serious injury.

■ If fording a river which is not in heavy flood, it is useful to use a stout stick as a third leg. It must be inserted on the upstream side and can be used as a probe for depth.

■ Never face downstream where the force of the water acting on the back of the legs can cause the knees to give way. Make sure that one foot is firmly placed before moving the other. Do not cross your legs. Shuffle the feet; don't lift them up.

■ It can be a great help to angle the hips in such a way that the current exerts a force in the direction of crossing. Adopt a 'ferry-glide' position with the leading hip (i.e. the one nearest the bank you are heading for) advanced to make an angle of up to 45° with the current.

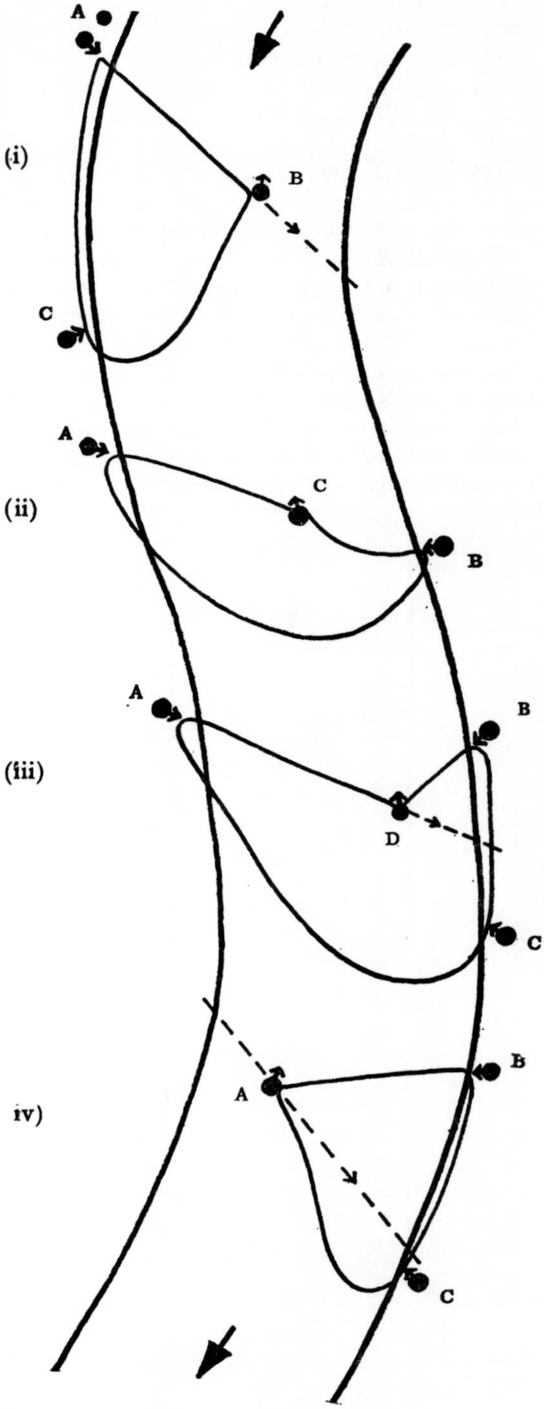

(i)

(ii)

(iii)

iv)

Fig. 12: **Crossing with a rope**

Method using a rope
(*See illustrations*)

Fig. 12 The leader 'B' ties on to a loop in the rope (figure of eight knot) and sets off across and slightly downstream supporting himself on the rope held by 'A'. He should face upstream at all times. 'A' and 'C' should not be belayed and simply pass the rope through their hands. In the event of 'B' slipping in, he is pulled to the shore by 'C' while 'A' lets his rope run.

Never try to pull a man to the bank from upstream of him. He is certain to be dragged under.

(ii) On reaching the far bank 'B' slips off his waist loop but leaves it tied to the rope. 'C' ties on to a second loop and, supported by 'A', who should, if possible, take up a position on a suitable promontory, sets off in the manner described for 'B'. If 'C' should fall in he is pulled to shore by 'B', on the downstream side.

(iii) Once two men are established on the far bank the method can be varied slightly to assist those who come after. 'B' can now take up a position upstream of 'D', crossing, and offer him considerably more support with the rope. Should 'D' fall in he can still be fielded by 'C' on the downstream side.

(iv) The last man crosses in a similar manner to the first, supported by 'B' and pulled in by 'C' if he falls in.

Fig. 13. If two ropes are available the leader and second man may cross as in (i) and (ii) above. The third ('D') and subsequent members of the party tie on to the middle of one rope and the

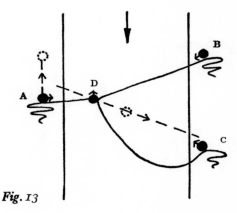

Fig. 13

end of the other as shown. 'D' is supported by both 'A' and 'B' as he crosses diagonally downstream. In the event of a mishap he can be fielded by 'C'. On reaching the far bank he unties and secures the rope from 'B' and 'C' to the 'tail' held by 'A'. 'A' then pulls all the ropes across for the next man.

Fig. 14. Alternative method of getting main body across when high banks or trees permit a single rope to be stretched taut across the river.

The leader 'B' crosses in the manner previously described, tying on to two ropes instead of one.

On reaching the far bank he unties and one of the ropes is stretched taut across the river diagonally downstream as shown and some 10 ft. to 12 ft. above the surface. Any solid anchor can be used, such as a tree or rock, provided it gives sufficient clearance. The rope can be tensioned by 'A' and the remainder of the group using a simple pulley system.

It is important that it should be tight enough not to sag into the water when holding the weight of a man at its mid point.

'C' then ties on to the middle of the second rope held by 'A' and 'B' on opposite banks. He attaches himself to the taut rope by means of a sling (or loop in his safety rope) and karabiner. For stability, he can hold on to the fixed rope and assisted by 'B' makes his way diagonally downstream to join him. The remainder of the party cross in the same way with the exception of the last man who crosses in a similar manner to the first.

The method is effective and safe if properly rigged, but is dependent on finding suitable

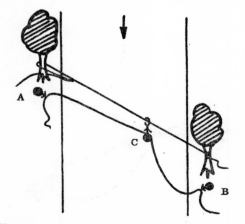

Fig. 14

anchors in the right position and high enough above the river. The party must also be carrying two ropes, karabiners and slings.

Method without a rope

Only in circumstances of the most dire necessity should any attempt be made to cross a river without a link to the bank. In such circumstances the following methods have proved to be the most successful:

■ Cross in groups of three with arms firmly linked, heads close together and feet apart. The lower man must face upstream and only one must move at a time. In this way the two stationary men can support the moving man.

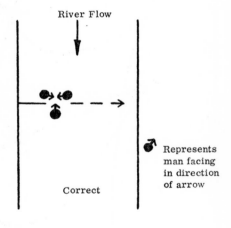

Correct

Represents man facing in direction of arrow

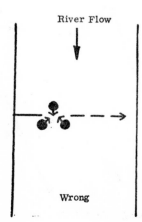

Fig. 15

Wrong

■ A satisfactory alternative method is for three or more to cross in a line downstream thus:

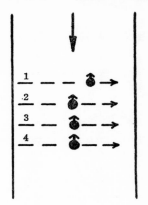

Fig. 16

The first man takes a small step sideways, supported by No. 2 who should be the heaviest in the party. No. 2 steps into line behind him, supported by No. 3 and so on until all the party are in a single line downstream. No. 1 moves again and the process is repeated. In this way the line moves slowly across the stream. In heavy water it is better if the group moves as a single unit (i.e. all take a step at the same time).

If either of these methods is used great care is absolutely essential.

6 Exposure—causes and avoidance

Introduction

In recent years a great deal of attention has been focused on 'exposure'. An understanding of the subject among mountaineers has been greatly facilitated by the publication of the findings of the Outward Bound working party appointed in 1963 to report on the dangers, detection and treatment of exhaustion and exposure on mountains. I am grateful to them for permission to quote from their report in this Chapter and also to Dr. Gordon Waddell for permission to reproduce the Expedition Chart, Fig. 19.

In the past few years there has been a significant increase in the number of reported cases of exposure. No doubt this is in part due to the increased numbers at risk and to improved knowledge leading to recognition of its symptoms, but it is also the result of a vast increase in the number of officially sponsored parties of young people taking to the hills. All too often these youngsters are badly equipped and led by people who are woefully ignorant of the basic rules of mountain safety and who themselves lack the relevant experience to cope adequately with any emergency. On the whole, young people are particularly sensitive to exposure. Their physical and mental reserves are less than adults and for this reason great care must be taken in the planning and execution of any expedition to ensure that they are not over-stretched. There is, perhaps, some danger that our attention may be diverted from the bread and butter business of prevention by the spectacular recommendations on the treatment of exposure cases. Many long cherished cures have been thrown out the window along with St. Bernard dogs, brandy and hot-water bottles. Think ahead. There is no substitute for careful planning.

Definition of exposure

This is not a strict medical term but in general usage it describes the serious effects which may result from exposure to climatic hazards. It is, in general, limited to the effects of cold environments, phrases frequently used including 'suffering from exposure', 'death by exposure', 'risk of exposure'. The essential feature of conditions described in this way is a reduction in the heat content of the body. This becomes serious when deep body temperature begins to fall. So, a definition of exposure to meet the current use of the term is: Severe chilling of the body surface leading to a progressive fall of body temperature with the risk of death from hypothermia.

The importance of exhaustion in the exposure syndrome cannot be overemphasised. It is this factor which distinguishes exposure in the mountains from other forms, such as that suffered by old people in winter in inadequately heated houses or by immersion in the sea. In these cases the cause is almost entirely confined to the cooling effect of the environment. In the mountains, cold alone rarely kills, but when the energy reserves of the body are so depleted that it can no longer maintain deep body temperature, exposure is the sequel.

It is the combination of exhaustion, cold, anxiety or mental stress which is especially dangerous. The elements in this combination will vary greatly with the individual, as will the individual's susceptibility to some or all of these factors. In considering exposure to cold, it is well to bear in mind what was written by the late Mr. D. G. Duff, F.R.C.S., himself a mountaineer and rescuer of long experience. 'It is, I consider, the additional factor of physical exhaustion over and above cold which kills quickly. Death has overtaken whole parties who, thinking they must keep moving at all costs, have "bashed on" instead of resting in some shelter before exhaustion supervened. The essential is always to preserve a sufficient reserve of energy in severe conditions of cold and high wind.'

As a rider it may be added that, as with an injured and immobilised climber in the mountains, it is clear that cold may kill a person who is not, as such, physically exhausted. In this condition, however, the climber would certainly be suffering from shock and would therefore be much more susceptible to the effects of cold. Everything should be done to minimise shock and to allay his fears. It is emphasised that the risk of death from exposure is a real, and often unrecognised danger among those, particularly the young, undertaking mountain expeditions in bad weather conditions.

Causes of exposure

The causes of exposure may be divided into two categories: those factors which relate to the *individual* and those which relate to the *environment*.

Environmental Factors

■ In the dry cold environment the factors to be considered are air temperature and wind speed, the combined cooling effect of which is known as wind chill. For any given air temperature the cooling effect (wind chill factor) increases rapidly with increasing wind speed. This is most marked at lower wind speeds, so that, in the range 0 – 15 m.p.h., even small changes in wind speed can have a profound effect on the degree of cooling. At wind speeds above 15 m.p.h. the factor changes more slowly. This does not mean that high winds can be discounted in other respects. A great deal of extra energy is obviously required to fight against a 60 m.p.h. wind than a 15 m.p.h. one.

It is possible to express the degree of cooling as a number, but out of doors, this has little meaning. It is of more practical value to know what the equivalent temperature would be in still air, for all possible combinations of wind and temperature. The graphs in Fig. 17 allow

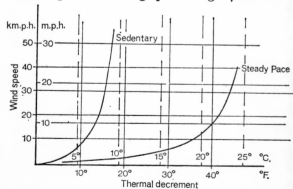

Fig. 17

The thermal wind decrement to be subtracted from the shade temperature to give equivalent still-air temperature. Note that it depends on the amount of work being done. (Burton and Edholm, 1955).

such calculations to be made. Notice, particularly, how the number of degrees to be deducted, to arrive at the still-air temperature, varies with the amount of work being done. The more strenuous the effort, the greater the cooling effect.

To take one example: the shade temperature is 10°C (50°F) and the wind speed is 15 m.p.h. If the party is stationary, then 8°C (14°F) must be deducted from the shade temperature to arrive at the equivalent temperature in still air. This is, therefore, 2°C (36°F). If the party is going at a steady pace, 23°C (41°F) must be deducted, giving an equivalent still-air temperature of −13°C (9°F). If strenuous exercise is being taken 32°C (58°F) must be deducted, giving an equivalent still-air temperature of −22°C (−8°F).

In the matter of prevention then, protection of the whole body from the wind is important.

■ Most cases of exposure in the mountains of the United Kingdom occur in wet cold conditions and it is astonishing that in a country with such a high annual rainfall more attention has not been directed towards remaining dry. Even the best clothing suffers an enormous loss of its insulating efficiency when it becomes saturated, and in a wind, heat loss is further accelerated by convection and evaporation. Complete waterproofing brings its problems, but these can, at least in part, be overcome by good design.

Individual Factors

INSUFFICIENT OR INADEQUATE CLOTHING
It follows from the above that clothing should offer a reasonable degree of independence from the environment. A *waterproof* anorak (and therefore also windproof) is a 'must' and there are many reasonable, cheap, lightweight 'cagoules' on the market. Beware of garments that 'breathe' – few of them stand up to practical testing and in really wet conditions they leak at the seams and under the rucksack straps. If an anorak of this type is worn then a waterproof over-anorak must be carried in the pack. Sweating can be a problem, but the design should allow for a considerable degree of ventilation and this keeps condensation to a minimum. Careful regulation of pace uphill and of the amount of clothing worn helps to avoid discomfort. In dry cold conditions the clothing assembly, including the anorak, should be vapour permeable, to allow insensible water loss from the body to evaporate. If both wet and dry cold conditions are likely to be encountered, then some combination of a permeable inner and a waterproof outer garment is essential.

A comprehensive list of clothing and equipment for different expeditions in summer or winter is listed in appendix 'E'. It is however worth drawing attention to the fact that an enormous amount of heat can be lost from the thighs and also from the head, both parts of the body that are all too commonly ignored as far as adequate cover is concerned. Jeans are quite unsuitable for outdoor work and give absolutely no protection in bad weather. The range and design of protective clothing nowadays is such that it is inexcusable for groups to set out inadequately clad. It is the instructor's or leader's responsibility to see that each person in his charge is wearing or carrying sufficient to afford adequate protection in the event of bad weather.

LOWERED RESERVES OF ENERGY
leading to exhaustion. This may be caused either by attempting too much or by not replacing used energy by eating sufficient food. Exhaustion in itself is a dangerous condition since it implies that the body is quite unable to mobilise any further reserves of energy either to do physical work, in other words to carry on, or even to maintain normal body temperature against the sapping of the environment. A man engaged in heavy manual work expends something between 4000 and 4500 kilocalories per day. The mountain equivalent of this is a 12-mile walk involving 2500 ft. of climbing. In fact a fairly normal sort of mountain day. The calculation is based on a simple formula. (G. Waddell 1965):

$$E = 100 (10 + R + 2C + 4H)$$

where E is the energy expenditure in kilocalories per 24-hour period; R is the distance travelled on roads in miles per day; C is the distance travelled across country in miles per day; and H is the total height climbed in thousands of feet per day.

Quite clearly, an expenditure of the order of 4400 kilocalories of energy per day is going to require good training and an adequate food intake especially if this level of output is to be maintained for any length of time, as on an expedition for example. The formula, too, does not make allowance for difficult terrain, weather and load carried, all factors which could add substantially to the total energy demands. There are of course energy reserves available in the body but you cannot go on drawing on them indefinitely – sooner or later they have to be topped up by a period of rest and recuperation. A good balanced diet providing about 4000+ kilocalories per day is essential and this should include a high energy lunch snack to be taken on the hill in addition to the personal emergency ration which of course must be kept in reserve. Over a period of time routes and expeditions should be planned so as to avoid making excessive overall demands, especially on young people. Start in a modest way with expeditions in the 2400 – 2800 kilocalorie range and gradually build up to more ambitious projects. Exhaustion is always a possibility, but it becomes a probability if routes demanding more than 4500 kilocalories are tackled without

½ hour for each 1000 ft. climbed. However, it takes no account of terrain, weather, load carried, fitness, and the effect of fatigue at the end of a long day. In fact for short or long trips it is wildly out. Recent modifications to Naismith's rule have attempted to take account of as many of these variables as possible. The results of this work are tabulated below (Tranter 1965). Fig. 18.

The left-hand column represents varying degrees of fitness or condition (with the fittest at the top) as measured by the time taken when fresh to climb 1000 ft. in ½ mile at a 'normal' pace and without rests. Once the individual fitness rating is known or estimated it is possible to read off from the chart the 'corrected' value for any time calculated on the basis of Naismith's rule. Other adjustments are necessary to take account of the remaining variables.

■ Distance on Roads: in calculating time

Corrections to Naismith's Rule

Time taken in hours calculated according to Naismith's rule

Individual Fitness in Minutes	2	3	4	5	6	7	8	9	10	12	14	16	18	20	22	24
15	1	1½	2	2¾	3½	4½	5½	6¾	7¾	10	12½	14½	17	19½	22	24
20	1¼	2¼	3¼	4½	5½	6½	7¾	8¾	10	12½	15	17½	20	23		
25	1½	3	4¼	5½	7	8½	10	11½	13¼	15	17½					
30	2	3½	5	6¾	8½	10½	12½	14½								
40	2¾	4¼	5¾	7½	9½	11½										
50	3¼	4¾	6½	8½												

Too much to be attempted

Limit Line

Fig. 18: Corrections to Naismith's Rule

adequate preparation and training. Know the individual capabilities of your party and plan accordingly.

The estimation of time to be allowed is of vital importance both in navigation and in route planning. Naismith's rule has for long been enshrined in mountain lore as the basis for all these calculations – and rightly so since it gives approximately the right answer for an average party on an average day, i.e. 3 m.p.h. plus

according to Naismith's rule work on the basis of 4 m.p.h.
■ Load Carried: drop one 'fitness' line from the one normally used for each 30 lbs. carried.
■ Terrain: drop one or two 'fitness' lines according to the nature of the ground. Under snow the time taken varies enormously, depending on its state at the time. Once this has been established drop 1 – 4 'condition' lines as appropriate.

■ Weather: drop one 'fitness' line at night or in bad visibility or if strong winds are present. If strong head winds are forecast for the return journey drop two 'condition' lines.

This rather involved process of arriving at a fair estimate of the time required for any particular journey has been neatly summarised in the chart – Fig. 19. (Aldridge, Waddell,

about 4 pints per day, but in a hot climate and when engaged in hard physical work it can rise to five times this amount. There is a general reluctance among walkers and climbers to take water on the hill. This seems to be due to vague fears of pollution, stomach cramps and other debilitating effects, most of which are imaginary. Water is required and the more work done, the

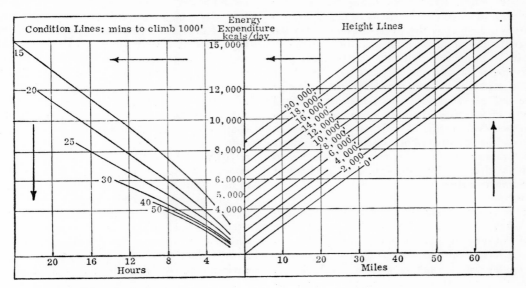

Fig. 19: Expedition time chart

Tranter.) Start at the bottom right-hand side of the chart with the 'corrected mileage', i.e. the total mileage across country plus three-quarters of the total distance on roads. Follow the arrow vertically until you intersect with the line representing the total height climbed. From this intersection move horizontally towards the centre line and read off the Energy expenditure. Continue leftwards to meet your particular 'Fitness' line; adjusted of course to take account of the factors previously mentioned, i.e. Load, Terrain and Weather. If you run out of 'Fitness' lines it can be assumed that conditions are too severe. If you do not meet your line because it stops short the trip must also be regarded as too arduous. From this point descend vertically to the base line to read the estimated time in hours.

DEHYDRATION

Perhaps because water is so plentiful in Britain we tend to ignore the fact that it is a vital ingredient of the diet. The normal turnover is

more water is necessary. Roughly speaking about ¾ pint is required for each 1000 kilocalories of energy expended in winter and about double this in summer. The 12-mile mountain walk involving 2500 ft. of ascent previously referred to demands an expenditure of 4400 kilocalories and a water requirement in summer of 6¾ pints. It is of course possible to go into water debt and replenish stocks at the end of the day, but if the expedition is a long one this could be a dangerous policy. It is better to keep pace with the needs of the body and drink when the opportunity presents itself, 'little and often' being the best maxim to follow. On a long expedition salt lost through sweating should also be replaced to avoid muscle cramp. Serious dehydration leads to a decrease in physical and mental efficiency and lowers resistance to exhaustion.

LACK OF TRAINING AND CONDITIONING

The importance of training and of a gradual

build up towards more ambitious expeditions has already been stressed. Overestimation of fitness and underestimation of time are all too common causes of accidents. Where large groups are concerned it is obviously better to arrange people into fitness groups according to their condition times than to cater for all on the basis of the lowest common denominator. The latter policy, apart from being bad for the morale of all concerned, leads to the dangerous situation whereby the weak can be pushed too far and the strong barely kept at 'tick-over'.

In addition to improving the physical performance of individuals, training should be designed to familiarise the group with the range of difficult conditions which may be expected and in this way condition them to a certain extent both mentally and physically against hardship and discomfort. Such conditioning is of proven value in cold climates and there is no doubt that it helps to maintain a high level of morale in our own.

MORALE

This is something of an unknown quantity. Certainly it cannot be measured and yet it is one of the most significant contributory factors to exposure. Apprehension, fear and a spirit of hopelessness can induce a state which, if not checked, can spread through a party like a bush fire. Apprehension itself, is of some short term benefit in meeting a difficult situation, since its effect is to increase the activity of certain organs of the body, including the heart. However, if this keyed-up condition is sustained for a long period, it drains the energy resources of the body and leads to exhaustion. Furthermore, the improved peripheral circulation results in cooled blood being returned to the core, and in this way accelerates the loss of body heat. Confident and cheerful leadership should be the keynote with a wary eye and ear for the first sign of depression or panic. This does not mean that in a tricky situation the leader should pretend that everything in the garden is lovely but rather that he should inspire the confidence and the willingness to co-operate among his charges that is necessary for a successful outcome.

INJURY

Shock is present to some degree in every case of injury and it is important to treat the patient for this as well as for his injuries. A person in a state of shock is much less able to combat the effects of cold and maintain his body temperature. He is in fact half way towards exposure already and must be protected from the environment by all means at your disposal.

7 Exposure—recognition and treatment

Symptoms of exposure

It is not always easy to decide early enough that you have a mild case of exposure on your hands. It is very important to do so, since it may be possible to avoid a crisis if at the outset you are aware of the symptoms and can begin to treat them. This makes it incumbent on the leader to know his party sufficiently well to be able to recognise genuinely uncharacteristic behaviour when it arises.

The following are among the symptoms:
■ Unexpected and apparently unreasonable behaviour, often accompanied by complaints of coldness and tiredness.
■ Physical and mental lethargy, including failure to respond to or to understand questions and directions.
■ Failure of, or abnormality in vision. It should be noted that some failure of vision is a very usual symptom, and when this does occur, the condition should be regarded with extreme seriousness.

■ Some slurring of speech. There is not necessarily early *failure* of speech and victim may speak quite strongly until shortly before collapse.

■ Sudden shivering fits.

■ Violent outbursts of unexpected energy – possible physical resistance to succour – violent language.

■ Falling.

N.B. It should be stressed that not all of these symptoms may be noticed, nor necessarily in this order. Other symptoms which may sometimes be observed are muscle cramp, extreme ashen pallor, light-headedness, occasionally a fainting fit.

Treatment

General

In normal conditions the inner 'core' (trunk and brain) of the body remains constant at 37°C (98·4°F): the temperature of the outer shell consisting of the skin, underlying fat and muscle, and extremities (arms and legs, ears, nose) is always below this.

What is vital is the preservation of the deep core temperature. A shift in this leads directly to *mental deterioration and loss of muscular co-ordination, and eventually to unconsciousness, heart and respiratory failure and death.*

The body itself acts to maintain core circulation and temperature by restricting the flow to the exposed periphery so that core blood is not cooled at the surface.

In any treatment, therefore, the importance must be realised of not increasing peripheral circulation unless there is minimal loss of heat at the skin surface, further heat loss from the core must at all costs be avoided, sudden local surface warming therefore is wrong.

When once the symptoms are clearly established, any further exertion, such as forcing the victim to go on walking, even downhill, must be avoided. The party must stop, and proceed to treatment. *It is impossible to overstress the importance of this.*

Immediate Treatment in the Field

As already indicated, the risk of precipitating a sudden surge of circulation to the surface, such as may be produced by hot water bottles / rubbing / or alcohol intake, should be avoided.

The precipitation of a sudden surge of core blood can be disastrous, as this blood is cooled by going through the cold outer shell, and is then returned to the heart.

The essential and immediate treatment is to prevent further heat loss by insulating the body and to use every means available to make a positive contribution to the heat balance of the victim.

Methods will vary according to conditions and the equipment immediately available. An outline of what should be done, if at all possible is:

■ If plenty of dry insulation is available remove the victim's wet clothes, dry him, and get him into a sleeping bag. If this is impracticable, wrap him in sleeping bags to provide insulation below as well as above his body.

■ Put a fit companion into the sleeping bag alongside him, to give him bodily warmth.

■ There should be a windproof and waterproof covering (e.g. polythene) around the bag and the victim. The insulation between him and the ground is most important.

■ Try to provide some shelter as windbreak.

■ Meanwhile, get the rest of the party to pitch a tent over the victim to provide fuller shelter. If the tent has a sewn-in groundsheet, carry him inside the tent. Light a stove if carried and get as many people inside as possible, but ensure adequate ventilation.

■ If the victim can still take food, sugar in easily digestible form (e.g. condensed milk) may be given. A warm sweet drink may be prepared later if available.

■ If respiration ceases, perform artificial respiration continuously by mouth to nose / mouth method.

■ Be alert for failure of the heart (no pulse, blue lips, dilated pupils) and commence cardiac massage immediately. If necessary a second person can continue resuscitation at the rate of one inflation after every five compressions.

There will then normally ensue a period perhaps of some hours duration, before the rescue party with stretcher that has been summoned can arrive. Even if, during this period, the patient apparently recovers, and even if he insists that he is quite fit, he must still be treated as a stretcher-case, however unwilling or ashamed he may be, and the full normal rescue drill must be enforced. During this waiting period, once the patient has been insulated, a brew-up should be started, and hot beverages and food should be given to him, according to what he can take. Food and hot drinks should also be taken by those members of the party who have remained with him, and whom it is safer to regard as themselves suffering in some degree from shock and exhaustion.

The stretcher party, when it arrives, should of course preserve all the insulation around the patient, during the carry, with which he has been protected during the waiting period. It is important that his face and mouth should be protected, to minimise heat-loss, without interfering with ventilation and ease of breathing. It is imperative that in descent the patient should be evacuated in the head down position and that someone (not a stretcher bearer) is detailed to keep an eye on him in case of vomiting, respiratory or cardiac failure.

If a case of exposure occurs in a very distant and isolated spot, and the delay before the arrival of the rescue party is likely to be inordinately long, the instructor or leader may face the very difficult decision as to whether to start removing the casualty towards the rescuers and safety. But before any such attempt is made, all the measures of immediate treatment in the field, as outlined above, should be taken first. And only if considerations of time, distance, and bad weather then clearly make it less of a risk to carry the patient towards safety, than to keep him, insulated and cared for, where he is, should the risk of carrying him be accepted.

This emphasises the real need for all instructors and leaders in charge of a party to be trained not only in up-to-date First Aid methods, including mouth to nose resuscitation, but also to be expert in the safest carrying techniques that may be attempted without a proper stretcher.

Recommended Treatment at Base

If it can be done, rapid rewarming by total immersion in a hot bath between 113°F and 117°F or 45°C and 47°C is a proved lifesaver. A bath thermometer is a useful thing to have available, otherwise judge the safe heat as being the hottest temperature in which you can keep an elbow in the water. A bed and room should be warmed while the bath is being prepared. Strip the patient, at least of wet outer garments,

and immerse in the bath taking care to exclude any frostbitten part. This should be dealt with separately (see Chapter 16). The legs too may be left out (Gramminger) since a suffusion of blood in that direction may dangerously reduce the blood volume. The bath temperature will drop immediately and therefore it must be topped up with hot water at regular intervals. After 20 minutes, or when the patient begins to sweat, remove him in the prone position (do not sit him up) and transfer to the previously warmed bed. Recovery is often spectacularly misleading. Insist on complete rest and examination by a doctor as a matter of urgency.

Such sophisticated facilities will not be available in a base camp. However, much the same effect can be achieved in a superheated tent (ensure adequate ventilation) and by immersing both hands in a billy of water brought to the same temperature (113°F – 117°F).

There is no doubt that rapid rewarming, effective though it has proved, involves a certain degree of risk, especially for the unconscious, the very old and the very young and in others who for one reason or another are frail or unwell. It is suggested that in such cases spontaneous rewarming in a warm room and bed (no pillow) should be the treatment of choice.

Conclusion

It is said that an Eskimo, immersed in cold Arctic water, will die from hypothermia (cooling) just as quickly as the rest of us. His ability, not only to survive, but to live comfortably in a hostile environment is almost entirely due to the fact that he keeps fit, dresses well and is highly experienced in avoidance. This, perhaps slightly unfair comparison, sums up all that is necessary to know as regards prevention. Better by far that you should know how to avoid getting a case of exposure than to cure one. Therefore:

■ See to it that the equipment and clothing worn by the party is sufficient for the route chosen and takes cognisance of sudden and unexpected changes in conditions. Water-proofing is a must whether it be worn or carried in the pack.

■ A minimum of emergency food and equipment must be carried by the party. In winter time, at high level, this may include a lightweight, bivouac tent, sufficiently large to accommodate the whole party. A suggested list may be found in Appendix E.

■ Adequate food and water should be taken before and during any mountain journey.

■ Progressive training is important as is the careful regulation of pace throughout the day. Arrange large groups according to their fitness and capabilities.

■ Loads in excess of 40 lbs. are unnecessary, as well as being heavy. As a rough guide on a camping expedition loads should never exceed one-third of the body weight of the individual.

■ Good morale means increased safety.

■ Safety first – seek shelter or turn back in good time.

■ Good leadership is good planning.

Finally it must be said that good leadership is also an awareness on the part of the leader of each member of his party as an individual; an awareness amounting almost to a premonition of possible hazards and dangers that may arise and above all the ability to take avoiding action before circumstances dictate their own terms.

8 Effects of heat

It is often said that man is a tropical animal, and it is certainly true that in general it is a good deal easier to lose heat than to conserve it. However, in a cold climate, heat conservation is achieved by the relatively simple expedient of improving the insulation, whereas, in a hot climate, heat loss is largely controlled by physiological adjustments which are outside the control of the individual. It is easier to wear an overcoat than a refrigerator. Exposure to heat is, in any case, a rare phenomenon in this country. However, cases of quite serious sunburn and mild heat exhaustion have been known, and the mountain leader should be familiar with the main heat disorders and their avoidance.

WATER REQUIREMENTS

Since most of these disorders are due to water depletion, rather than the direct effects of heat, an appreciation of the water requirements of the body is necessary. As a rough guide, $2\frac{1}{2}$ litres may be taken as the average daily requirement, broken down as follows:

	ml per 24 hours
Urine	1400
Respiration	400
Insensible perspiration	600
Faeces	100
Total	2500 (5 pints)

This figure is greatly increased by hard physical work, especially in hot weather, when an additional 750 ml ($1\frac{1}{2}$ pints) may be required for every 1000 kilocalories of energy expended. Most of this water is evaporated as sweat, and in this way, serves to cool the body surface. The evaporation of 1 litre of sweat (2 pints) results in a heat loss of about 600 kilocalories. In really hot climates the water requirement may be as much as 14 pints/24 hours.

SALT REQUIREMENTS

Normally our salt intake is a good deal more than our actual requirements, but prolonged sweating can lead to substantial salt losses, particularly in those who are unacclimatised. Fortunately, acclimatisation to salt depletion in a hot environment takes place fairly rapidly and the immediate effects can be countered by the simple expedient of taking salt, solid or in solution, and by cutting down on water intake.

ACCLIMATISATION

Very little is known about long-term adaptation to heat and one is left with the impression that, as with the eskimo in the cold environment, experience in avoidance is the best protection against the harmful effects of a hot climate. There is no doubt that short term adjustments take place in a matter of several days of exposure to heat and these include:

a less marked increase in heart rate when working, a lower skin and deep body temperature, greater efficiency of the sweating mechanism (sweating is more rapid in onset), a reduction of salt in sweat and urine and a marked increase in tolerance of the conditions.

SUNBURN

This can be very severe particularly to those with sensitive skins. In addition, sunburn can interfere with sweat secretion and lead to further heat complications. It is usually caused by sudden and prolonged exposure to sunlight without adequate protection. The length of exposure should be carefully regulated to build up a protective tan and initially, at any rate, an efficient barrier cream used which does not interfere with sweating and which cuts out most of the harmful ultra violet radiation. In applying the cream it is important to remember the lips and also those areas of the face which receive a lot of reflected light from the ground or snow, under the nose and ears, chin, etc. Sunburn can be effectively treated with calamine lotion.

EFFECTS OF GLARE

Snow blindness is considered briefly in the winter section (page 101). Here we are concerned with discomfort and strain, as a consequence of inadequate protection of the eyes. The remedy is simple; wear sunglasses. These must be of good quality and reduce the amount of ultra violet without cutting down too much on the total transmission of light. In snow conditions, especially at high altitudes, it is essential to shield the eyes as well from light entering round the sides of the lenses.

Heat disorders

PRICKLY HEAT

This is an irritating rash of tiny blisters, usually caused by constant sweating in a hot climate. The only real cure is to get out of the sun and rest, although various measures can be adopted to relieve the symptoms.

HEAT SYNCOPE

Unacclimatised people exposed to heat frequently suffer periods of acute fatigue associated with fainting or a feeling of giddiness. This is a common condition and it can be counteracted effectively by rest.

HEAT EXHAUSTION

When due to water depletion, this can be a very serious condition, leading ultimately to death.

The symptoms include, thirst, fatigue, giddiness, a rapid pulse, raised body temperature, low urine output and later on, delirium and coma. The only remedy is to re-establish water balance.

When due to salt depletion, similar symptoms are manifest though without any marked rise in body temperature, but almost always associated with severe muscle cramp. It can be serious if not treated by the addition of salt to the diet. There is no such thing in man as a craving for salt and therefore the victims are unaware that they are suffering from a deficiency.

HEAT STROKE

Mistakenly referred to as sunstroke. This is by far the most serious of the heat disorders and is caused by a failure of the body's temperature regulating system. It is associated with a very high body temperature and the absence of sweating. The skin is hot and dry to the touch. Early symptoms show a remarkable similarity to the symptoms of exposure, such as aggressive behaviour, lack of co-ordination and so on. Later on the victim goes into a coma or convulsions and death will follow unless effective treatment is given.

In the field, the treatment consists of sponging down the patient, or covering him with wet towels, accompanied by vigorous fanning. It is imperative to begin treatment immediately, unless of course, the shortage of water is so acute that other lives may be endangered. When facilities permit, immersion in a cold bath (10°C or 50°F) is the treatment of choice.

PRECAUTIONS

It is wise to remember that it is not possible to acclimatise to a low intake of water. A certain minimum quantity is required for survival. Most of the recommendations, therefore, concern conservation of water.

■ Keep fit. Fitness is very important, especially when travel is involved.

■ Do the minimum of work consistent with the achievement of the expedition's aims.

■ Keep out of the sun as far as possible and certainly during the hottest part of the day.

■ Drink more than you need when water is readily available. Thirst is a poor indicator of your actual requirement and a reserve will be useful on a long journey.

■ Don't hoard water till collapse is imminent.

■ Be prepared to collect rainwater by tapping as large a surface area as possible e.g. with a polythene sheet. A plastic straw can be used to extract water from rock pools.

■ A high calorie diet, short on protein, is desirable.

■ Wear loose, lightweight clothing, permeable to sweat and light in colour. Also a shady hat and sun glasses. On no account labour uphill in hot conditions with fully waterproof clothing.

9 Weather

Introduction

An ability to understand, interpret and anticipate weather changes is desirable for any mountaineer; for the Mountain Leader, that ability is essential. It is as important as good route planning, or ropehandling, or knowledge of equipment. The knowledge must be practical, so that it can be used and it must be built on an understanding of what the Mountain Leader has observed and experienced. The British Isles have changeable weather that can bring snow in summer and mild days in winter. Although these inconsistencies give an impression of unpredictable conditions, the available short-term (i.e. day to day) forecasts are reliable; also, the knowledge required to anticipate weather changes in the mountains is not great. An understanding of a few basic principles, together with habitual observation of everyday weather, is all that is required.

Background Knowledge

From the mountaineer's point of view, weather has several important elements:
temperature, cloud, precipitation (humidity), and wind.

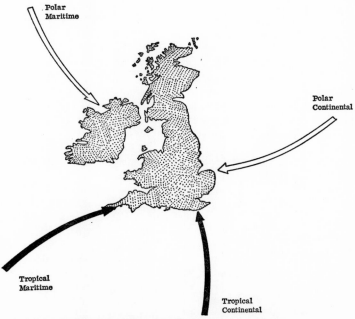

Fig. 20: Major airstreams which are liable to affect the British Isles

Weather occurs in the atmosphere and the air behaves as a gas. So, the main points to remember are that:

(*a*) cooled air – *contracts – sinks – sheds moisture.*

(*b*) warmed air – *expands – rises – carries more moisture.*

Also, air is warmed or cooled primarily by conduction (i.e. touching something warmer or cooler) and convection (i.e. mixing); it is not warmed by radiation (i.e. by direct sunlight). So, the temperature of the air and the amount of moisture in it (giving cloud, rain or snow) is determined before it reaches you, the observer. Consequently, if you know where the air is coming from, you can make a forecast.

Air that remains in contact with the earth's surface gradually acquires properties, notably temperature and humidity, of the underlying surface. The regions where these air masses are found are called air mass sources and Britain is near the junction of these. From these source areas air flows out gently and this forms the airstreams which together account for a large part of British weather.

The four major sources and the characteristics of the airstreams are:

■ *Tropical Maritime.* S.W. winds fairly steady. Warm and moist, even in winter. Stratus cloud forms on the West side of mountains often with rain or drizzle but generally the weather is clear and dry on the lee side.

■ *Tropical Continental.* Winds S. or S.S.E. Hot and dry. Very poor visibility in summer. Clear skies but hazy. This airstream is not common, but it can bring very high winter temperatures.

■ *Polar Maritime.* N.W. winds. Cold in winter and cool in summer. It is an unstable airstream

with showers developing frequently particularly to windward of mountain ranges. Cumulus and cumulo-nimbus cloud form is typical. Except in showers there is very good visibility. See Fig. 21.

■ *Polar Continental.* North and north-east winds. The weather is cold and dry. Conditions are unstable and therefore showery with cumulus clouds but the air lacks moisture and in winter the phenomenon of ablation is common (i.e. snow falling but apparently disappearing as it reaches the ground).

Depressions and Anti-cyclones

These systems are recognisable to the observer by the weather they bring and may be drawn on charts by considering the barometric pressure. Atmospheric pressures are recorded at weather stations and then lines are drawn on the chart joining places of equal pressure. These lines are called isobars and they form patterns that allow us to see Depressions, Anti-cylones, Fronts and wind strength and direction.

A depression is an area of relatively low atmospheric pressure. Some of the smaller depressions, or lows, usually with associated fronts (a front is the junction between different types of air), move quickly and generally exhibit certain features of cloud, wind, temperature and humidity which are easily recognisable.

The winds in all depressions in the northern hemisphere blow anti-clockwise and slightly inwards, across the isobars. The closer the latter are together, the stronger the winds. From the diagram, Fig. 22, it can be seen that if an observer stands with his back to the wind, low pressure is on his left. This is always true and is an aid to determining the observer's position in relation to pressure distribution.

By observing wind direction, it is possible to recognise various stages in the passage of fronts and of the depression. If, for example, (see fig. 22) a depression moving from W. to E. passes over an observer standing at X, the sequence of wind change would show a veering (wind change in the same direction as the movement of the sun) from S.W. to W.S.W. as the warm front passed and to the W. with the passage of the cold front. If, on the other hand, the track of the depression passed over an observer at Y, then the initial wind would be S., followed by light winds and then a sudden veer to the W. The passage of fronts is heralded by cloud

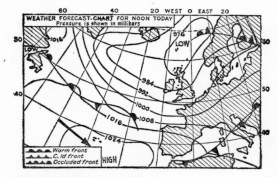

Fig. 21: Maritime airstream

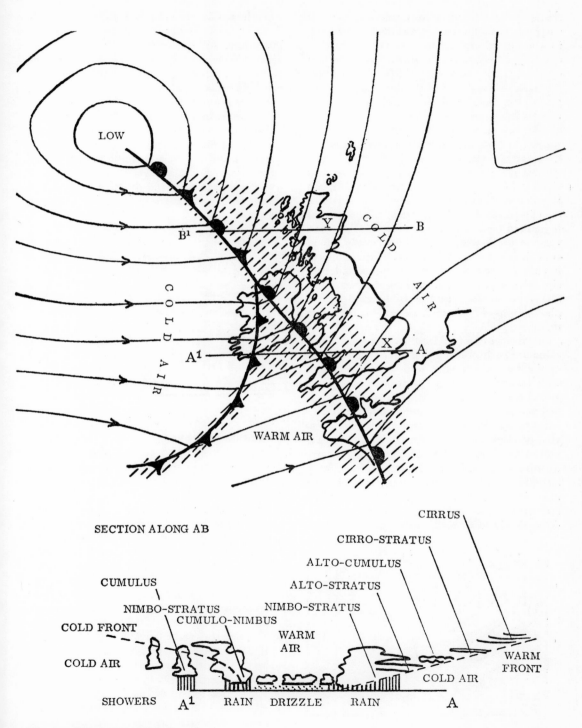

Fig. 22: Depression with fronts

change. Well ahead of a warm front, small wisps of cirrus increase in amount, developing into a veil of cirrostratus. With this type of cloud the phenomenon of a halo round the sun or moon is not uncommon. Closer to the front, the medium height cloud thickens and falls to a lower altitude. This altostratus cloud continues to thicken and eventually, as rain begins to fall, it becomes nimbostratus (rainstratus). As the warm front passes, the surface wind veers and frequently stops, or gives place to a drizzle. At this stage it is not unusual for the stratus cloud to break up and expose clear sky, although low stratus cloud with continuous light drizzle is equally possible. The passage of the cold front is marked by a fall in temperature. The wind veers to north-west and, simultaneously, cloud cover breaks to expose blue sky. The cloud form is cumulo-nimbus and alto-cumulus and precipitation is in the form of heavy showers. (The books on weather in the Bibliography have photographs of clouds. Learn to recognise them).

The passage of a cold front or of a warm front alone are both possible, but over Britain much of the rain which falls does so in association with an occluded front (warm and cold fronts joined together). This gives rise to very modified warm front or cold front characteristics.

Figure 23 shows an anti-cyclone or a large area of High Pressure centred slightly to the east of the British Isles. This type of pressure distribution, shown by isobars, brings fairly static weather conditions. Light winds blowing in a clockwise direction and even dead calms are characteristic and changes, when they occur, do so slowly and usually over a period of days.

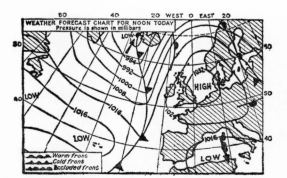

Fig. 23: Anticyclone

Cloudless skies are often associated with anti-cyclones, but overcast conditions are not infrequent. In both summer and winter, overnight temperature inversions (i.e. lower temperatures near the ground) are fairly common and, particularly in sheltered inland valleys, there are often frosts and fog.

Conditions in a Ridge of High Pressure (Fig. 24) are not unlike those in an anti-cyclone but they are normally of shorter duration. In a fast moving ridge it is often possible to locate one's approximate position in relation to the system by reference to the wind direction and by this means crude estimations of further changes can be made.

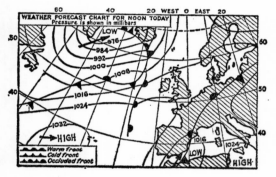

Fig. 24: Ridge of high pressure

Mountain Influences

The weather experienced over the country in general is further modified by the mountains. The three main modifications are:

1. Atmospheric Pressure

   Air pressure at the top of mountains is less than at the bottom. Air flowing over them will therefore be forced into an area of lower pressure and will expand and cool. In cooling, it can hold less moisture, so extra rain and cloud develop on the tops. However, on the lee side of a mountain area, the descending air increases in temperature and clear periods are more frequent.

2. Temperature and Sunshine

   If the air is well mixed the air temperature decreases with altitude:

   2°C/'000 feet in humid air
   3°C/'000 feet in dry air.

   If the sea level temperature is 6°C, for example, the temperature at 3,000 feet will be at freezing point or even colder.

If the air is still, cold air will sink into valleys to give cold pools, or frost hollows. The temperature is lower than on the tops; this is called a temperature inversion and is common in anti-cylones. Because there is little dirt and moisture in the air, on a clear day the direct sunlight at 4,000 feet is bright, containing twice the ultra violet light that is experienced at sea level.

3. Wind Speed

Wind is the movement of air to equalise atmospheric pressure. At sea level, because of friction, winds are gusty, but of reduced strength. At high altitudes they are very much stronger and steadier. Knowledge of wind speed is important and vitally so in winter conditions, where even a light breeze can reduce the environmental temperature (i.e. the temperature as it is felt by the human body) to an uncomfortable level. The wind speed on open land above 3,000 feet is about two to two-and-a-half times stronger than on more sheltered low-lying land and, for example, a strong breeze of 23 to 27 miles per hour, would become a gale or storm of 50 to 60 miles per hour at the higher open altitude. Environmental temperature is also affected by humidity. The 'raw' conditions of winter and the 'mugginess' or 'oppression' of a sultry summer's day are all too common. At the other end of the scale a south easterly airflow can have a dessicating effect on people and vegetation.

Personal Forecasting

Personal forecasting is a product of using one's background knowledge to modify and update existing available information. Forecasts are available from the following sources:

(a) BBC/ITV Television. These give general forecasts, with up-to-date weather maps.

(b) Newspapers. All give some sort of forecast. Some papers give two maps – one of which is a forecast map, and the other a report.

(c) Radio. At various times throughout the day the BBC transmits detailed regional forecasts. Information about these can be obtained from 'Meterological Office Services Weather Advice to the Community. Met. Office. Leaflet No. 1, H.M.S.O.' With practice, it is possible to plot an up-to-the-minute weather map using information transmitted on the BBC long wave shipping forecast. Outline maps (Met. Maps) for this purpose are obtainable from the Royal Meteorological Society, Cromwell House, High Street, Bracknell, Berks. RG12 1DP. Guidance in constructing these maps is contained in a booklet – 'Your Own Weather Map' by I. E. Wallington.

(d) Meteorological Centres. These may be contacted by telephone (addresses are listed in 'Weather Advice to the Community') and are in the best position to give up-to-date forecasts, with extra information about freezing level, cloud base and so on.

To develop weather knowledge, follow this procedure:

1. Listen frequently (at least once every day) to the weather forecast. Listen for key words which might herald bad mountain weather: for example; Front, Trough, Depression, Low Pressure, Falling Pressure, Increasing cloud/wind.

Conversely, the following words frequently suggest good mountain weather: Calm or light winds, High Pressure, Anti-cyclone, Rising Pressure, Clear skies, Fog and/or frost warnings.

2. Read the daily weather forecast and then deliberately observe the weather. Get to know what is meant by 'showers and bright intervals', 'cloud spreading from the west', 'Gale, Force 8', 'continuous heavy rain', and other phrases commonly used to describe the weather.

At the same time, try to identify clouds by reference to pictures. (*Cloud Study*. A Pictorial Guide prepared under the auspices of the Royal Meteorological Society, by F. H. Ludlam and R. S. Scorer.)

3. Having practised the above for some weeks, try looking at weather maps and making a forecast before reading the text. Check with given forecast.

4. Having practised (3), try to make forecasts by observing the weather first. Check your opinion against maps and text.

5. Having practised (4), don't look at the paper; just go out and make a forecast from what you can see and what you know has happened recently.

The key to all forecasting is to look into the

approaching weather. This applies equally to reading weather maps and anticipating what large changes may occur and also to looking into the wind whilst out walking in order to anticipate the next shower ten minutes before it arrives.

Although maps and regional forecasts give knowledge of the weather over a wide area, they nearly always refer to low lying ground. The ability to interpret the local mountain situation in the light of this information is a practical skill which all Mountain Leaders should cultivate.

10 Lightning

Lightning can hardly be regarded as a major mountain hazard yet every year it claims the lives of two or three mountaineers. Like the winter avalanche it is commonly regarded as an Act of God and the very impartiality by which it chooses its victims encourages a fatalistic outlook among climbers and walkers. The actual physical process is now fairly well understood and this emphasises that there are certain simple precautions which can be taken to avoid a strike.

The first thing to realise is that to be 'struck' by lightning is by no means always fatal. True,

a direct hit is likely to be so, but more often than not the victim receives only a part of the stroke, either by induction because he happens to be standing near, or through the ground in the form of earth currents which dissipate like the roots of a tree, from the source. Such partial shocks need not be fatal though they could, of course, cause death indirectly if the climber should fall off or be rendered incapable of fending for himself. The stroke itself is a variable quantity, being a product of a very large current (thousands of amps) and a very short time

Frequency of Strokes:

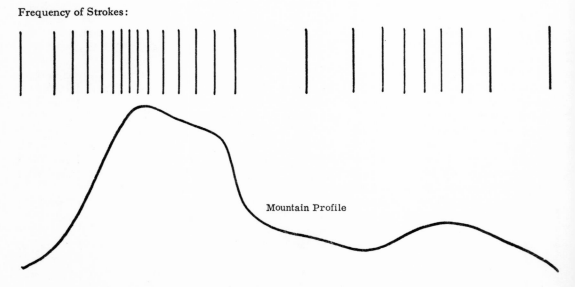

Mountain Profile

Fig. 25: Frequency of 'strokes' in mountain area

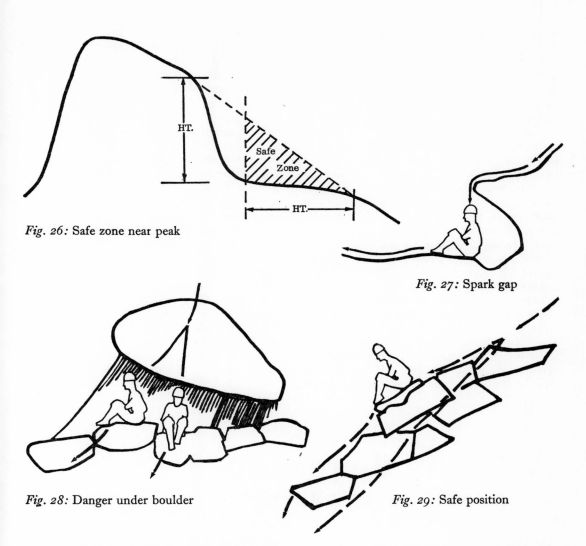

Fig. 26: Safe zone near peak

Fig. 27: Spark gap

Fig. 28: Danger under boulder

Fig. 29: Safe position

(thousandths of a second). In many cases a much smaller current in contact for a few seconds could cause considerably more damage.

Fortunately there is usually some advance warning of the approach of an electrical storm and avoiding action can be taken, but once in the firing line decisions tend to be taken out of your hands. Anyone who has experienced the literally hair-raising preliminaries will vouch for this. Ice axes hum and spark, the skin tingles and local projections glow with a bluish light.

During a storm strikes tend to be concentrated on mountain tops or other natural projections from the general surroundings. At the same time, since such points 'service' a fairly wide area, there tends to be a shaded or relatively safe zone associated with them. The peak must be at least 20 ft. high and the relatively safe zone is of the same order horizontally (Fig. 26). Note that it affords no protection to be tucked in against the cliff or peak itself since in this position you are likely to receive earth currents shed from the peak.

The natural inclination in a really heavy storm is to seek shelter, especially if rain is driving down. Unfortunately, this is quite the wrong thing to do unless you can find a cave which gives you at least 10 ft. head room and 4 ft. to either side. Such caves and hollows in the rock are often simply local expansions of natural fissures. These in turn are the likely conduits for earth currents, especially if they hold water and by sheltering in them you are offering yourself as a convenient alternative to the spark gap. (Figs. 27 and 28).

Exactly the same argument applies to sheltering under large boulders. With reasonable waterproof equipment remaining dry should not be a major problem and it is much safer to sit it out in the open. Try to find a broken scree slope, preferably in a safe zone and sit on top of a *dry* rope or rucksack with your knees up and your hands in your lap (Fig. 29). Do not attempt to support yourself on your hands or by leaning back. The object of these precautions is to keep your points of contact with the ground as close together as possible and in such a position that a current flowing along the ground would tend to pass through a non-vital part of the body.

On a cliff face sit out the storm on the nearest ledge, but avoid chimneys and fissures of any kind. If a belay is necessary, try to avoid using the wet rope as a natural lead from a vertical crack to your body. On an exposed peak or ridge your position is much more serious and it is normally advisable to make some attempt to get at least part way down even at the height of the storm. Abseiling in an electrical storm is a risky manoeuvre, but it is normally preferable to a position on the lightning highway of an exposed ridge. In any event, one or two rope lengths may well take you to a position of relative safety. If you do abseil, use a dry rope if you have the choice and use a safety rope. Fatal accidents have often resulted from a non-fatal strike which in the first instance has merely stunned the victim.

It is fashionable, too, to discard pieces of extraneous equipment; cameras, rucksacks, crampons and even ice axes, under the mistaken impression that they 'attract' lightning. They don't, any more than you do yourself. The electrical resistance of the average wooden shafted axe between head and spike is almost five times that of the human body. If it is humming and sparking it may be prudent to lay it down carefully beside you, but no more. The axe is much too valuable a tool to be tossed away in a storm. It may well be needed to deal with icy rocks on the retreat.

11 Mountain rescue

If you are the leader of a party involved in an accident

■ *Don't rush.* See to it that no immediate danger threatens the victim or the rest of the party.

■ *Render immediate first aid* and reassure the victim and the remainder of the party.

■ *Make the victim as comfortable as possible* and provide warmth and shelter as far as circumstances and equipment allow. Be particularly careful to provide adequate insulation from the ground. Provided the victim is not suffering from a spinal injury it may be advantageous to move him to a more sheltered site. If this is not possible then build shelter round him.

■ *Decide on your course of action.* In making your decision weigh carefully the following factors:

The nature of the victim's injuries / The state of the remainder of the party / The time available / The weather situation / The availability of assistance / The evacuation route.

■ *Attempt to attract local assistance using recognised distress signals.*

The table below lists the internationally agreed signalling code. It should be borne in mind that a single signal can easily be missed. Repeat until acknowledged. Thunder flashes etc. may be used to attract attention. White flares are also used for illumination.

Either

■ *Send a messenger for help or, if a party of two, go yourself.*

The messenger should carry a written note

giving: precise location of the accident – six-figure map reference and compass bearings from known landmarks (if on a climb, the name of the climb and whether near the top or bottom); time of accident; number involved; injuries sustained.

If the victim is to be left on his own he must be told to 'stay put' at all costs. He should be given all the spare food and clothing and provided with a whistle and torch if these are not required by the messenger. Mark the spot clearly with a flag – a brightly coloured garment held on top of a cairn of stones. The climbing or safety rope, if not otherwise required, may be extended out from the victim to act as a marker guide. Remember that the rescue party may have to find the exact spot in the mist or in the dark and in winter the victim may well be covered with drifting snow. An unconscious patient must never be left alone. If a party of two, it is safer for the uninjured person to stay with the victim to render help when necessary

and to attempt to attract the attention of other climbers and walkers. Only as an absolute last resort should the victim be left and in that event he should be tied securely to the rock if in an exposed situation and a note left explaining what action has been taken. It is worth remembering that an injured person will normally attempt to untie himself.

Or

■ *Arrange to evacuate patient(s) yourself, improvising equipment as necessary.*

At the outset it should be remembered that improvised 'carrys' and 'stretchers' are of short range value. It would be exhausting and possibly dangerous to attempt a long evacuation by such methods. Their main use is in moving an injured person to a more sheltered situation or in evacuating someone with relatively minor injuries or, of course, when evacuation by any method is preferable to leaving the victim where he is.

Message	Flare Signal	Audible Signal	Light Signal
HELP REQUIRED	Red Flare(s)	6 blasts etc. in quick succession, repeated after a 1 minute interval. SOS: three short, three long, three short blasts etc. in quick succession repeated after a 1 minute interval.	6 flashes in quick succession repeated after a 1 minute interval. SOS: Three short, three long, three short flashes, repeated after a 1 minute interval.
MESSAGE UNDERSTOOD	White Flare(s) (also used for illumination)	3 blasts etc. in quick succession, repeated after a 1 minute interval.	3 flashes in quick succession, repeated after a 1 minute interval.
RETURN TO BASE	Green Flare(s)	A prolonged succession of blasts etc.	A prolonged succession of flashes.
POSITION OF BASE	White or Yellow Flare(s)		Continuous light

Table of agreed signals used in Mountain Rescue.
N.B. FIXING POSITION. As soon as a signal is seen (or heard) a compass bearing must be taken on it. Two such bearings if taken from different positions, will give a reasonably accurate fix on the position of the signal.

IMPROVISATION

Fireman's Lift, two, three or four hands methods are unsuitable for distances over 50 yds.

Method:
  Piggy Back
People Required:
  One
Equipment & Means:
  Nil
Comment:
  Exhausting

Method:
  Rucksack Carry
People Required:
  One
Equipment & Means:
  Rucksack & padding. Casualty sits on padding, legs through rucksack straps
Comment:
  Good

Fig. 30: Rucksack carry

Method:
  One-man Split Rope Carry
People Required:
  One
Equipment & Means:
  Rope & padding. Casualty sits on padding within coils of rope
Comment:
  Not so comfortable

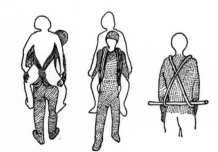

Fig. 31: One-man split rope carry

Method:
  Two-man Split Rope Carry
People Required:
  Two
Equipment & Means:
  Rope & padding. Split coils into two over outside shoulders of carriers. Casualty sits on rope (padded) in between
Comment:
  Not so good on rough terrain. Unstable fore/aft

Fig. 32: Two-man split rope carry

Method:
Two-man Rucksack (or Crossed Sling) and
Pole Carry
People Required:
Two
Equipment & Means:
Two rucksacks (or four slings) & pole or long
ice axe. Pole slotted through rucksack straps
(or crossed slings) behind carriers' back.
Patient sits in between on pole
Comment:
Uncomfortable for casualty

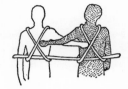

Fig. 33: Two-man sling and pole carry

Method:
Sedan Chair
People Required:
Three
Equipment & Means:
One rucksack, two poles or long ice axes, one
anorak. Anorak sleeves inside out, poles slotted
through to form seat. Front carrier wears ruck-
sack, poles slotted through straps. Casualty
sits back to back with front carrier. One
carrier either side at rear of poles
Comment:
Good

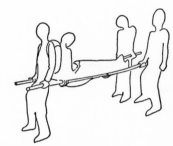

Fig. 34: Sedan chair

Method:
Full Length Sedan
People Required:
Four or more
Equipment & Means:
Long poles (tent), four anoraks. As above only
casualty lies prone. The bed can be made
with anoraks, tent, poly bag or rope
Comment:
Excellent. Rigid sides easier to carry

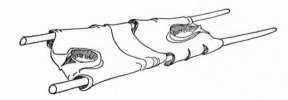

Fig. 35: Full length sedan

Method:
Modified Piggott Rope Stretcher

People Required:
Six or more

Equipment & Means:
12oft. of rope and plenty of padding. Overhand loops down one side joined with sheet
bend knots down the other side. Loops at
corners. Finish off down middle with a
series of overhand knots

Comment:
Hard work, but satisfactory if well padded
and plenty of carriers. Better with poles for
rigid sides

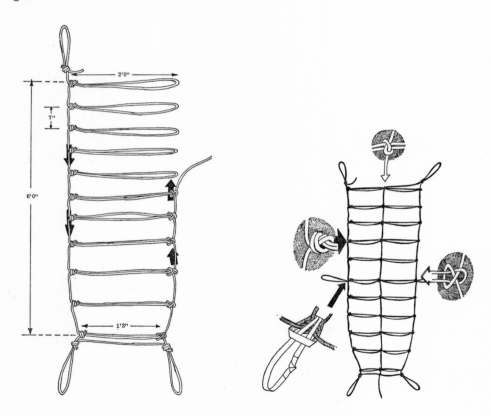

Fig. 36: Modified Piggott rope stretcher

Method: Alpine Basket
People Required: Six or more
Equipment & Means:

120ft. of rope. Rope laid on ground in a series of S bends (about 20in. wide at feet and 40in. at chest), loops pulled up round casualty and interlocked. Pad with poly bag and rucksacks, then use rucksack straps for carrying

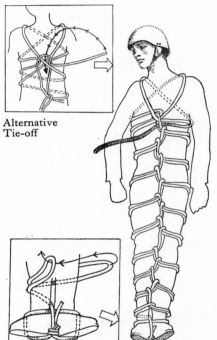

Alternative
Tie-off

Fig. 37: The alpine basket starting at the feet and lacing to the chest

Method: Triple Bowline
People Required: One
Equipment & Means:

This knot is tied on the doubled end of the rope. The three loops are placed round the upper thighs and one across the chest, over one shoulder. The knot should be high on the chest and the three loops should be tied together at the back with a tape or handkerchief

Comment:

Incorrect positioning of the loops and knot will result in a top-heavy posture, which could be dangerous. The method can be used to lower an injured or frightened person down a short difficult section

Comment:

Best for lowers. May be started at the feet and tied-off at the chest or started at the chest and tied-off at the feet

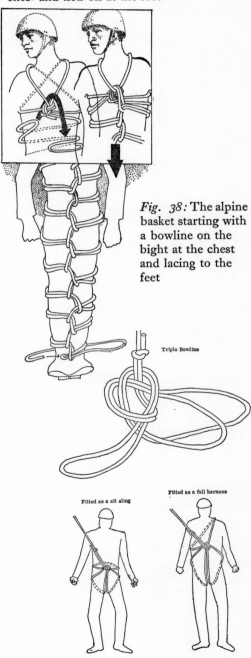

Fig. 38: The alpine basket starting with a bowline on the bight at the chest and lacing to the feet

Triple Bowline

Fitted as a sit sling

Fitted as a full harness

Fig. 39: The triple bowline

OTHER USEFUL KNOTS FOR RESCUE WORK:

Bowline on the Bight: Used as a chest harness to start the Alpine basket rope stretcher.

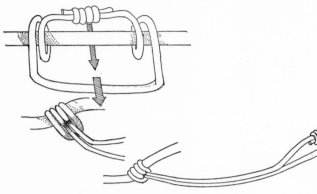

Fig. 40: Bowline on the bight

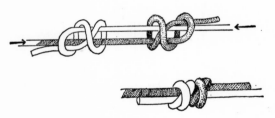

Fig. 41: The Prussik knot

Prussik Knot: This is a type of barrel knot which is used to attach a separate loop or line to the main rope, in such a way that the knot can be pushed up or down the rope, but will lock onto the main rope under load.

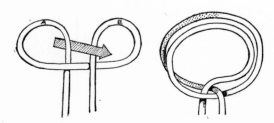

Double Fisherman Knot: Used to join two ropes.

Tape Knot: Used to tie nylon slings.

Fig. 42: The double fishermans knot

Clove Hitch: Used in conjunction with a bowline to attach lowering ropes to stretcher.

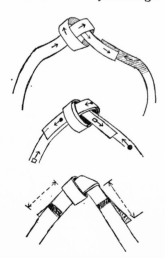

Fig. 43: The clove hitch

Fig. 44: The tape knot

Organisation of search

It is not expected that candidates for the Certificate will be concerned with the organisation of a major search and rescue operation. This is the responsibility of the local team leader in co-operation with the police. Nevertheless it is important that they should have a clear understanding of the system so that they can offer competent assistance in an emergency, perhaps as the leader of a smaller search unit.

Big searches are costly affairs, in terms of man hours as well as in hard cash. An efficient organisation makes the best use of all available resources, minimises delays and frustrations and greatly increases the chances of a successful outcome. Just as it is vital that each small group should have its appointed leader so it is vital that an experienced mountaineer should take overall responsibility for the control and conduct of the search. In a large scale operation this can only be successfully done from a fixed base in contact with all aspects of the search, both in the field and behind the lines.

1 Interview the person bringing the news of the accident. This is best done away from the crowd which invariably gathers at the mention of the word accident. On no account rely on second-hand information. This may be coloured and omit some vital piece of information concerning the circumstances.

2 Establish precise details of the accident, including location, time, number involved and the nature of the injuries.

3 Once this information has been given act *Speedily – Not Hastily. Inform the Local Police and Doctor*. He will make arrangements for an ambulance, but will require an indication of the expected time of arrival back at the roadhead.

4 Each area has devised its own call out system, but it is worth remembering that it is better to have a team on 'stand by' if there is any likelihood of their being required, than to call them out at the very last moment without warning.

5 No two search and rescue operations are ever the same and therefore the *plan* must be adapted to the circumstances. It should be drawn up immediately, again in consultation with the team leaders and the police. Contact the Meteorological Office for an up-to-date weather forecast and inform team leaders.

It is important that:

■ Team leaders are fully briefed on the circumstances of the accident and the responsibilities of their groups. Check on the experience and personal equipment of their members. Radio call signs and an agreed communications system should be established.

■ A record is kept, giving the names of the members of each party and their leader, the route to be followed, special equipment carried, radio call sign, time out, and expected time of return. This information could be of vital importance if a claim on insurance is to be made.

■ Each party should carry sufficient equipment to render positive assistance to any casualties, i.e. (i) first aid kit (ii) spare clothing (iii) food and drink (iv) the means to provide adequate shelter. Other equipment carried will obviously depend on the circumstances known about the accident.

■ *Night Search.* It is hazardous and a waste of man power to send all parties out on a general search at night unless fairly precise information is available. However, some immediate effort must be made and this should take the form of checking mountain huts and other known refuge points.

6 The Search

If the locality is known:

■ Send a small party ahead with an emergency first aid pack. Check that the morphia is in it, and that flares or radio sets are carried. This small first aid pack should contain sufficient materials to deal with most injuries. There is also tremendous psychological value in having help arrive as quickly as possible. If the stretcher party is inexperienced, as is probable, it is better to have the patients tidied up before the party arrives.

■ Organise a stretcher party to follow up the advance party. This should be at least twelve but preferably eighteen persons. Ensure that all members are properly clad and equipped. If there is any doubt, they should not be allowed to proceed.

If the locality is unknown, but the general area fairly well defined:

The stretcher(s) and other heavy gear should be left at some convenient advanced base where it is reasonably accessible to the various units. This base may be moved as the search progresses. Some teams, of course, will be carrying lightweight stretchers.

Three main methods of search are recognised and their use obviously depends on the number of searchers available, their experience, the nature of the ground and information available to the controller.

RECONNAISSANCE SEARCH

Small fast units consisting of three or four experienced men are sent out with the minimum of gear, with the object of locating the casualty as quickly as possible. Helicopters and dogs are tremendously useful in this sort of preliminary scouting operation and may save endless work later.

BLOCK SEARCH

This is the normal method of covering a fairly large area. Each team is allotted a piece of ground bounded if possible by natural features such as streams or ridges. It is then up to the team leader to choose the detailed method of search best suited to the terrain in his area. In most cases this will involve some sort of sweep in line across the area.

CONTACT SEARCH

This method, as the name implies, is designed to concentrate the search over a relatively small area, perhaps at the foot of a cliff or in an area where there is good reason to believe that the missing person may be found. The spacing between searchers is dictated by the ground and may vary from 50 yards in open country to one yard in thick bush. The important point to bear in mind is that this type of search should be conclusive. An area searched in this way must be clearly marked.

HELICOPTERS

These can be of immense value but their use is dependent on reasonable overhead conditions. When lives are at stake, sympathetic consideration is always given by the Service authorities to a request for a helicopter. Any such request should be made through the Police who will contact the Rescue Co-ordination Centre.

Here are some ways in which a ground party can assist the pilot:

■ Clear a level landing zone (LZ) approximately 20 yds. × 20 yds. of all loose material, sticks, etc.

■ Normally the clothing of the ground party should be sufficient to attract the attention of the pilot. If a marker of any kind is used it should be pegged down firmly in the centre of the LZ.

■ Indicate wind direction by releasing a smoke cartridge in such a position that it is on the

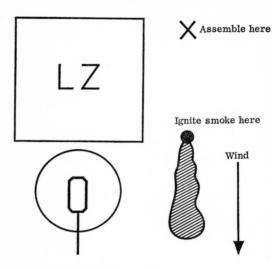

Fig. 45: Helicopter landing zone

pilot's right hand side as he approaches the LZ upwind. Ensure that the smoke will not obscure the LZ. If smoke is not available, then: stand with back to wind and arms outstretched facing the approach path, and shine a torch or headlamp into the wind, i.e. away from the approaching helicopter.

■ The ground party must assemble on the right hand side of the approach path and well clear of the LZ.

■ Approach the helicopter at 45° from in front and on the pilot's side so that he can see you.

■ Do not go near the tail rotor.

■ If a landing cannot be made a casualty may be lifted on the winch. Three methods are in common use: *single lift; double lift* (the casualty is assisted by the winch man); and *stretcher lift*. The casualty is placed in a Neil Robertson stretcher and lifted horizontally into the craft, assisted by the winch man. It is possible to lift other types of stretcher provided they are fitted with attachments to make a horizontal lift feasible.

There is an internationally recognised code of signals for ground to air communication. Here are just a few of the more important ones:

△	safe to land here
I	require a doctor
↑	proceeding in direction of arrow
X	unable to proceed
N'N	nothing found
II	require medical supplies
IIIII	require assistance
L'L	all well

USE OF DOGS

Possibly the best type of dog is the Alsatian, but many other breeds have done equally well. The only restriction really is on the size of the dog (it should be big enough to negotiate deep snow) and that it has a good nose. Generally the following breeds have been successful: Collies, Alsatians, Labradors, large Terriers; Dobermans, despite their short coat, also work well. Any cross breeding from the above list should also produce suitable strains. Long haired Alsatians have not proved successful.

To make full use of the Search & Rescue Dog Service, handlers should be allowed to search the most likely areas before large parties of searchers move in. This is especially easy at night when often searches are called off, or, in bad weather when it is impracticable for ordinary search work. Dogs should also be allowed to work into the wind and if the Search Organiser bears this in mind for the dogs, speedy recovery of the missing person(s) is often possible. As a rough guide a dog is equal to approximately 20 trained searchers, but in conditions where the victim(s) may be covered by snow its potential is much greater. You should bear in mind that dogs cannot work miracles, but when used properly can be a tremendous asset to any Rescue Team. Some dogs will find bodies even when partly frozen, but dogs' reactions vary and the handlers can advise in respect to their own dog.

For search and rescue work in Britain, dogs are classified as in other countries in three groups: 'A', 'B', and 'C'. The highest standard is 'C'. The British training differs from other countries and it includes summer searches. Dogs, if required, operate at a distance from their handler to cover as large an area as possible. Abroad, dogs are specifically used for close searching avalanches, whereas here their value lies in searching snow covered areas and open moorland, where the victim can be covered with a small amount of fresh snow or hidden in heather or hollows. Dogs of 'A' grading are subdivided from 1 – 10, 'A1' being the highest standard in the group. All 'A' dogs are suitable for searching moorland and easy mountainous regions in both summer and winter. If the letter 'M' is shown on the Certificate this denotes that the handler is a mountaineer and that he and his dog are capable of use in all conditions. Certificates are valid for two years.

An annual training and grading course is held in Glencoe each December.

For further information concerning the Search and Rescue Dog Association and for a list of available dogs and handlers write to:
K. MacKenzie, 1 Canal Road, Inverness.

7 Equipment

A full list of equipment held at official Mountain Rescue Posts is listed in the Mountain Rescue Handbook. Basically it consists of a stretcher and two rucksacks containing medical supplies, though certain Posts, especially those associated with local teams, carry a great deal more.

The main items to remember are:

■ Personal clothing and equipment. Refer to the kit list, Appendix E, but be particularly careful to ensure that you have adequate lighting. A pocket torch or head lamp may last less than one hour so take plenty of spare batteries. Long life cells are available.

■ Stretcher. There are many different types of stretchers, the Thomas, the MacInnes, the Duff, the Neil Robertson, the Akja from Austria, the Mariner and the Norwegian Helpe to mention but a few. Many of these are designed for a specific task or for a particular type of terrain. The Thomas is the standard issue for Mountain Rescue Posts in this country though many teams are equipping themselves with the new MacInnes – a hinged stretcher constructed out of continuous alloy tube with metal runners and wheel attachment.

■ Rescue rucksacks. These contain all essential medical supplies including three, quarter-grain ampoules of morphia – see instructions in the Mountain Rescue Handbook on when and how to administer and also for a list of the contents.

of the two sacks. They should be carried by the advance party if there is one. In the case of several search parties, each must carry sufficient material to enable it to render first aid to the injured.

■ Casualty Bag. Many posts and teams are now equipped with specially designed casualty bags incorporating sleeping bag, mattress and carrying handles. Their main advantages are that they allow minimal handling of the patient to get him into the bag, they provide a convenient method of transport to and from the stretcher and they offer excellent insulation from the ground or on the stretcher itself. Sleeping bags should be carried by teams not equipped with casualty bags (one is provided in the official kit).

■ Lightweight Tent. This is not part of the kit, but it could prove a life saver especially if the victim is suffering from exposure. On wide scale searches in bad conditions a tent with each team is a must. Some have designed a complete bivouac unit which will accommodate the whole team.

■ Search Lamps. At night each team should carry at least one search lamp capable of providing wide and narrow beam illumination continuously for at least four hours. It must be backed up by first class personal lighting and, if available, by illuminating flares.

■ Signalling devices. Very pistols, rockets, miniflares, thunderflashes and so on may be of use in favourable conditions. The agreed code is as follows: Red – help wanted here; Green – recall to base; White – message understood. Do not rely on a single flare. Release several at intervals till acknowledged. A thunderflash or other loud noise will attract attention before releasing flares.

■ Radio communications. Many teams are now equipped with portable transceivers. Most of these are on the Mountain Rescue frequency, but call signs and frequencies should be checked before departure and procedure, including time on and off the air, established. Good communications can be a tremendous asset in any search and rescue operation, but their maintenance should not so dominate the conduct of affairs that other vital considerations, such as speed and efficiency of search, are neglected.

■ Food and Drink. Adequate supplies of food and hot soup or other liquids should be carried to meet the needs of both rescuers and rescued. If the search is likely to be a long one then a stove, fuel, billies and the necessary material (tea, sugar, etc.) may ease the weight problem.

■ Specialised Equipment. Depending on the circumstances of the accident certain items of more specialised equipment may be required; climbing ropes, crash helmets, pitons, slings, karabiners and so on. In any event at least two ropes should be carried by each team since these may be required to deal with a host of unforeseen problems.

8   Evacuation of Victim

■ With the main party, proceed to the scene of the accident at a steady pace. Do not rush there as the time is being put to good use by the advance party making the patient comfortable and rendering the necessary first aid. Remember that there may be a long carry back and energy must be conserved. If there is the prospect of a very long carry make arrangements for a support party to bring food and drink.

■ On the way in examine the ground for the best evacuation route and mark if necessary.

■ The arrangement of the victim on the stretcher will depend on the nature of his injuries and the type of stretcher. Freedom from pain on the move should be the aim. Remember that a helmet may be necessary if steep ground or screes have to be crossed. Be particularly careful in the case of suspected spinal injuries and avoid any movement of the spine itself. Place the victim on the stretcher exactly as he is found – use padding as required.

■ Unconscious, exposed or seriously injured casualties are best carried in the 'head down' position with the head tilted to one side. Someone must always be in attendance in case of vomiting, cessation of breathing or other emergency.

■ A stretcher-bearing party normally consists of 16 – 20 persons working as two teams and changing shifts every 10 minutes or so depending on the terrain. A third team is useful if the carry is to be a long one.

■ If the route is not obvious and has not been previously marked someone should be sent ahead to select and mark the best line. This is, of course, particularly important at night.

9   It is the job of the Rescue Controller or of the Police to give information to the Press. If

asked, give the facts as you know them, but on no account divulge any information about the victims, their names and addresses and so on. These details will be given by the Police.

10 Report to the Rescue Controller on return to base.

11 The Mountain Rescue Committee and the Mountain Rescue Committee of Scotland keep a record of all accidents in the hills. It is important that a full report on every incident should be submitted to them.

Appendices: Summer Certificate

Appendix A: Scheme of training

The Mountain Leadership Training Boards provide a comprehensive scheme for the training and certification of leaders and instructors in mountaineering.

Mountain Leadership Certificate (Summer)* is intended to cover minimum competence in the technical skills required to take a party on walking and camping expeditions on UK mountains under normal summer conditions. It is appropriate, with these limitations, for all teachers, youth leaders and other qualified adults who are already committed hill walkers and wish to take young people on to the mountains and to show them how to enjoy their mountain walking with safety. It is not a mountaineering or an instructor's qualification.

Mountain Leadership Certificate (Winter) is concerned with the very exacting technical skills required for taking parties on to the Scottish mountains under winter conditions. It is equally appropriate elsewhere in the UK whenever similar conditions exist or may be expected. It is an obligatory qualification for candidates for the Instructors' Certificates, for whom it forms an essential part of the training requirements, but it is also open to those who, having gained the Mountain Leadership Certificate (Summer), seek this particular qualification only.

Mountaineering Instructor's Certificate covers essential aspects of mountain craft, including rock climbing. It is the appropriate technical qualification for those wishing to instruct school pupils and youth groups in mountaineering. It also provides the necessary general preparation for those wishing to train for the advanced qualification.

Mountaineering Instructor's Advanced Certificate is intended specifically for instructors employed full-time at mountain centres and elsewhere. A higher technical standard is required in all aspects of the syllabus than at Instructor level and in addition, detailed knowledge and experience of specific responsibilities arising at Mountain Centres.

In England, Wales and Northern Ireland this certificate is known simply as the Mountain Leadership Certificate. The term "Summer" is intended to emphasise that winter conditions with their special hazards which can arise at any time of the year in Scotland, are not covered by this certificate. While such conditions are much more rare in the other parts of the UK, they can and do arise, and the limitations of the Mountain Leadership Certificate must always be borne in mind in this respect.

All enquiries to –

The Secretary, The Scottish Mountain Leadership Training Board, Scottish Sports Council 1 St. Colme Street, Edinburgh, EH3 6AA (031-225 8411);

The Secretary, Mountain Leadership Training Board, Crawford House, Precinct Centre, Booth Street East, Manchester M13 9RZ.

The Secretary, Northern Ireland Mountain Leadership Training Board, The Sports Council, 49 Malone Road, Belfast, BT9 6RZ (0232 66 9519)

Appendix B: Mountain Leadership Certificate (Summer)

The Mountain Leadership Certificate (Summer) hereinafter referred to as 'the Certificate', covers training in the basic skills required to take a party on walking and camping expeditions in mountainous areas of the United Kingdom under normal summer conditions. It is intended as an essential requirement for teachers, youth leaders and other adults wishing to take young people on to the mountains and to show them how to enjoy their mountain walking with safety.

Requirements

The Certificate will be awarded to candidates who fulfil the requirements of the Scheme to the satisfaction of the Boards. *Basic Training and Assessment will be carried out only at Centres approved by the Boards*, as follows:

An approved residential Course of Basic Training of at least one week's duration. A planned series of at least four approved weekend Courses arranged by a Centre or Organisation may be accepted by the Boards as being a Basic Training Course. A weekend will consist of two full days' activity.

A period of at least one year after Basic Training throughout which practical experience in mountaincraft is gained during weekends and holidays. Details of *all* experience will be recorded in an official personal Log Book which must be presented at assessment.

A residential week of Assessment during which the candidate will be tested in accordance with the Requirements and the Syllabus. The examination results, together with a report on the personal qualities and leadership ability of the candidate will be submitted to the appropriate Board by the Director of Assessment.

Minimum Age Limits

For entry to a Basic Training Course – 18 years.
For the award of a Certificate – 20 years.

Textbooks

All candidates are required to be conversant with 'Mountain Leadership' the official handbook of the Mountain Leadership Training Boards; 'Safety on Mountains'; 'Mountain and Cave Rescue'.

These publications are available from the following sources:
The Scottish Sports Council, 1 St. Colme Street, Edinburgh, EH3 6AA.
The Sports Council, 49 Malone Road, Belfast, BT9 6RZ.
The British Mountaineering Council, Crawford House, Precinct Centre, Booth Street East, Manchester M13 9RZ.

The Course of Basic Training

Basic Training will be given in the following subjects:
1   Map and Compass
2   Route Planning
3   Walking Skills
4   Personal Equipment
5   Camping Equipment
6   Campcraft
7   Security on Steep Ground
8   River Crossing
9   Special Mountain Hazards
10   Weather
11   Accident Procedure
12   Information on Clubs and Guide Books
13   Responsibilities of Party Leader
14   Related Interests

1   Map and Compass
■ Map Scales.
■ Conventional Signs.

■ Map References – The Grid.
■ Methods of showing relief
■ Contours – description of ground from information on the map.
■ Topographical features.
■ Measurement of distance.
■ Calculation of speed of movement over varying terrain with and without loads – Naismith's Rule.
■ Setting of the map – without compass.
■ Navigation across country with map but no compass.
■ Types of compass.
■ Methods of obtaining Grid and Magnetic bearings.
■ Plotting a compass course from the ground and from the map.
■ Method of obtaining a position fix by resection (back-bearing).
■ Navigation across country with map and compass especially in poor visibility (e.g. at night).
■ Hints on natural wayfinding (e.g. use of sun or stars).
■ Methods of teaching simple map and compass work to beginners.

2. Route Planning
■ Choice of Route.
■ Preparation of Route Cards – Bearings/Distances covered/Time taken.
■ Selection of campsites.
■ Expedition rationing.
■ Escape routes.
■ Bad weather alternatives.
■ Sources of Aid (telephones, M.R. Posts, etc.).

3 Walking Skills
■ Individual skills – pace, rhythm, foot placing, conservation of energy, balance and co-ordination.
■ Party skills – leader and tailman, psychology of the group, corporate strength.
■ Party procedure on different terrain, e.g. scree, narrow ridge, steep broken slopes.

4 Personal Equipment
Personal equipment required for mountain expeditions both high and low level, and in *all* weather conditions. Information given should stress the effects of wind, temperature and humidity as well as providing information on design, construction and types of material; care and maintenance of equipment.

5 Camping Equipment
■ Knowledge of the use of different types and makes of: Tents/Sleeping Bags/Stoves/Rucksacks and other light-weight camping equipment.
■ Knowledge of the principles of packing and loading personal and communal equipment.
■ Care and maintenance of camping equipment.
■ Knowledge of items required on given types of expedition, e.g. high level/low level, long duration/short duration camps.

6 Campcraft
■ Camp organisation and siting.
■ Tent organisation and siting.
■ Camp Daily Routine.
■ Hygiene on camp.
■ The Country Code.
■ Camp foods and cooking.
■ Use of Mountain huts and bothies.

7 Security on Steep Ground
The small amount of rock climbing included in the course is not intended to train leaders as rock climbers. Its purpose is to familiarise candidates with elementary techniques, to enable them to appreciate the limits of what should be attempted by a party without rock climbing experience, to recognise difficulties and potential dangers of terrain and to give competent help in cases of emergency. Any safe method of rope management will be accepted at Assessment, but the method used and taught should involve the use of the rope alone. It is emphasised that the techniques advocated here are not necessarily those which would be suitable for rock climbing. The following points will be dealt with:
■ Practice of movement on rock.
■ Ropes and rope management: tying-on; waist belay; belaying and interchange of belay.
■ Decision taking on steep, broken ground. Route selection, roping up, choice of belay, negotiating loose rock, etc.
■ Use and limitations of hillwalking safety rope (minimum length and weight of nylon

rope – 120 ft. of No. 3 or 9 mm Kernmantel).
■ Use of rope as a handrail and for linking party together, in appropriate circumstances.
■ Abseiling with safety rope.

8 River Crossing

When and when not to ford rivers followed by practice in:
■ Methods of finding the best crossing points.
■ Methods of crossing with and without line.
■ Skills and safety precautions to be practiced by the individual – method of progression. use of 'third leg', procedure with a pack, reduction of resistance or friction, danger from trees and snags.

9 Special Mountain Hazards

■ *Exposure* An understanding of the causes of the condition known as 'Exposure' or 'Hypothermia'/Recognition of the signs and symptoms exhibited by 'Exposure' cases/ Awareness of the basis for prevention of 'Exposure'/ Awareness of the methods of treatment of an 'Exposure' case – in the field, and at base.
■ *Frostbite* An understanding of the condition, its sign and symptoms, prevention and treatment.
■ *Lightning* An understanding of the probable distribution of strikes on a mountain, and of the probable flow lines or resulting ground currents.
■ *Heat Exhaustion* An understanding of the condition, its signs and symptoms, prevention and treatment.

10 Weather

An elementary knowledge of weather, for example:
■ Interpretation of the weather map recognising – areas of High Pressure/air flows (e.g. Northerly airstream)/depressions and frontal systems and weather normally associated with these.
■ Major cloud forms and associated weather developments.
■ Sources of information on weather, e.g. newspapers, radio/television broadcasts, RAF stations.

11 Accident Procedure

Candidates must have practical ability and theoretical knowledge in depth of the following:
■ Procedure in the event of an accident.

■ Methods of search and evacuation.
■ Equipment contained in M.R. Posts and Boxes.
■ Improvised Mountain Rescue Equipment – application and limitations.
■ Rope Seats.
■ Rope Stretchers.
■ Sleds.

12 Details of Clubs, Organisations, etc

■ Details of organisations providing training in mountain activities.
■ Details of Clubs, etc. willing to accept young people as members. Guide Books, etc.

13 Responsibilities of Party Leader

A thorough knowledge and awareness of the function and responsibilities of the party leader.

14 Additional Interests

A Mountain Leader should be knowledgeable about some or all of the following subjects:
■ Geology, Natural History, History of Mountaineering, Photography.

Practical Experience

to be gained between Basic Training and Assessment.

Practical experience must be gained over a minimum period of one year, during which:

1 The candidate shall obtain, prior to Assessment, a current adult Certificate in First Aid, as issued by the British Red Cross Society, the St. Andrew's Ambulance Association, the St. John's Ambulance Association or the Armed Services First Aid Certificate.

2 A record shall be kept in the Log Book of every expedition accomplished within the period. These should include not less than 16 days spent in mountainous country. At least half of this time should involve camping. As a guide, it is suggested that candidates should have climbed about thirty named peaks of 2,000 ft. – 3,000 ft. in more than one mountain area.

3 Every opportunity should be taken of practising the skills learned at Basic Training, i.e. map and compass work, campcraft, etc. Further practice in rock climbing should only be taken under expert guidance.

4 Candidates are encouraged to obtain some practice in leading and instructing small parties of novices in easy hill country.

Note

■ Candidates will be expected to know and conform to the points listed in 'The Country Code'.

■ Through observation of land form and of indigenous wild life, there can be a greater appreciation of mountains. The Boards recommend that on all expeditions, candidates become aware of the great natural interests of the countryside.

■ Special note will be taken of expeditions which the candidate has carried out in winter conditions, also any help given at rescue or search operations. Where practicable, as much experience as possible should be gained under expert guidance in conditions of snow and ice, but *note particularly* that this experience *is not essential* for the Summer Certificate. A high percentage of accidents occur as a result of slips on hard snow or ice and it is therefore important that no winter expeditions be undertaken without adequate training.

Assessment

Candidates are required to attend, at a centre approved by the Board, a final residential Week of Assessment.

Recommendation

The Director of Assessment will be responsible for submitting a written report on each candidate to the appropriate Board. This report will be compiled on the basis of examination results, etc., and with reference to a written report by the 'field assessor'. The latter must attend the expedition/camp since it is there that a candidate's qualities of leadership are most likely to be revealed.

The Director should regard marks obtained by candidates in written tests as a guide, and in coming to his decision should be confident that those recommended for the Certificate are competent to lead a party of novices in mountainous country within the limits set by the Scheme.

Exemption

Experienced persons may consider approaching a Board with a view to exemption from the initial training requirements in order that they may proceed more directly to assessment. Details and conditions for such exemption will be made available on application to the Secretaries of the Boards from whom information regarding courses and details of other Certificate Schemes may also be obtained.

Appendix C: Select Bibliography

This bibliography has been compiled to help those who are seeking to improve their all-round mountaineering competence. Mountaineering has the richest literature of any sport and candidates are encouraged to read as widely as possible. Books out of print are marked 'O.P.' but may often be found second-hand or obtained from libraries. Some country libraries have themselves good mountaineering bibliographies covering worldwide activity. This is a practical guide and not intended to be comprehensive.

Mountaineering technique

Bell, J. H. B.: 'A progress in mountaineering', (Oliver & Boyd), O.P.
Blackshaw, A.: 'Mountaineering', (Penguin), a comprehensive guide to technique.
Burns, W. C.: 'A short manual of mountaineering training', (Mountaineering Association).
Disley, J.: 'Tackle climbing this way', (Paul).
Evans, C.: 'On climbing', (Museum Press), O.P.
Francis, G. H.: 'Mountain climbing', (Teach Yourself Series – E.U.P.), O.P.
Kirkus, C.: 'Let's go climbing', (Nelson).
Langmuir, E. D. G.: 'Mountain Leadership', (Scottish Sports Council).
Lovelock, J.: 'Climbing', (Batsford).
MacInnes, H.: 'Climbing', (S.Y.H.A.).
Murray and Wright: 'The craft of climbing', (Kaye).
Peacocke, T. A. H.: 'Mountaineering', (Black), O.P.
Raeburn, H.: 'Mountaineering art', (Unwin), 1920, O.P.
Robbins, R.: 'Basic rockcraft', (La Siesta Press, California), 1971.
Styles, S.: 'Modern mountaineering', (Faber); 'Getting to know mountains', (Newes).
Unsworth, W.: 'Book of rock climbing', (Barker), 1968.

Wright, J. E. B.: 'The technique of mountaineering', (Kaye).
Young, G. W.: 'Mountain craft', (Methuen), O.P., A classic.

Camping, walking, equipment

Balsillie and Westwood: 'Mid moor and mountain', (Boy Scout Association).
Brathay Exploration Group: 'Handbook for expeditions', 1971.
Cox, J.: 'Camp and Trek', (Lutterworth); 'Lightweight camping' (Lutterworth); 'The Hike book', (Lutterworth).
Department of Education and Science: 'Camping', Education pamphlet No. 58, (H.M.S.O.).
Duke of Edinburgh's Award Scheme: 'Expedition Guide'.
Know the game: 'Camping', (Educational Productions Ltd.).
Schools Council: 'Out and about', (Evans, Methuen Educational).
Williams, P. F.: 'Camping and hill trekking', (Pelham).

Map and compass

Bygott and Money: 'An introduction to Mapwork and Practical Geography', (University Tutorial Press).
Disley, J.: 'Orienteering', (Faber).
Fenn, E.: 'Maps – How to read and make them', (Brown, Low and Ferguson).
Gatty, H.: 'Nature is your guide', (Collins).
Know the game: 'Map reading', (Educational Products Ltd.), 'Orienteering', (Educational Products Ltd.).
Laborde, E. D.: 'Popular map reading', (C.U.P.)
Mustard, C. A.: 'By map and compass', (Hugh Rees).

War Office: 'Military manual of map reading', (H.M.S.O.).

Maps

The Ordnance Survey one-inch maps are being replaced by the new 1:50,000 giving a welcome 25% increase in scale. Five special one-inch 'Tourist Maps' may be of interest to Mountaineers. These are: Ben Nevis and Glencoe, Cairngorms, Loch Lomond and the Trossachs, The Lake District and Snowdonia.

1:25,000 maps are available for most of England and Wales and Scotland with the exception of the Central Highlands and Islands. The Isle of Skye is however, covered by the Second Series (Sheet No. NG42/52 for the Cuillin Hills).

New style 'Leisure Maps' are being produced on the same scale. 'The Dark Peak' and 'The Three Peaks' are available at present.

West Col publish a 1:25,000 mountain map of the Lake District and Glasgow University a 1:35,000 Recreation Map of the Cairngorms.

For general planning, Bartholomews half-inch to one mile maps are excellent.

First aid and rescue

British Red Cross Society: 'Junior First Aid', (Educational Productions Ltd.); 'First Aid', (B.R.C.S., St. John and St. Andrew AAs.).
Edholm and Bacharach: 'Exploration Medicine'.
MacInnes, H.: 'International Mountain Rescue', (Constable).
March, W.: 'Improvised Mountain Rescue Techniques', (March, Glenmore Lodge).
Mariner, W.: 'Mountain Rescue Techniques', (Austrian A.C.).
Mountain Rescue Committee: 'Mountain Rescue and Cave Rescue', (Sports Councils and The Secretary, M.R.C., 9 Milldale Ave., Temple Meads, Buxton, Derbyshire, SK17 9BE); 'Practical First Aid', (Educational Productions Ltd.).
Royal Air Force: 'Mountain Rescue', (H.M.S.O.).

Weather

Forsdyke, A. G.: 'The Weather Guide', 1969, (Hamlyn, paperback).

Lester, R. M.: 'The Observer's book of weather' (Warne).
Ludlam and Scorer: 'Cloud Study', (Royal Meteorological Society).
Meteorological Office Services: 'Weather advice to the community': Met. Office Leaflet No. 1 (H.M.S.O.); 'The weather map', (H.M.S.O.). 'Elementary Meterology', 1962, (H.M.S.O.). 'Met. Maps' are obtainable from the Royal Meteorological Society, Cromwell House, High Street, Bracknell, Berks. RG12 1DP.
Schöpfer, S.: 'The Young Specialist looks at Weather', (Burke).
Scorer, R. S.: 'Weather', (Phoenix House).
Watts, A.: 'Instant Weather Forecasting', 1968, (Adlard Coles Ltd.).
Wallington, C. E.: 'Your own weather map', (Royal Meteorological Society).

General

Barker, R.: 'The last blue mountain', (Chatto and Windus), 1959.
Borthwick, A.: 'Always a little further', (Mackay).
Boel, J.: 'High heaven'.
Bonnington, C.: 'Anapurna, South Face'.
Brown, J.: 'The hard years', (Gollanz).
Buhl, H.: 'Nanga Parbat pilgrimage'.
Collomb, R. G.: 'A dictionary of mountaineering', (Blackie).
Clark, R. W. and Pyatt, E. C.: 'Mountaineering in Britain', (Phoenix House).
Crew and Wilson: 'The Black Cliff', (Constable).
Drasdo, H.: 'Education and the Mountain Centres', (available F. Davies, J. Brown).
Engel, C.: 'History of mountaineering in the Alps', (Allen and Unwin), 1971.
Fraser, C.: 'The avalanche enigma', (Murray).
Gray, D.: 'Rope Boy', (Gollanz), 1970.
H.M.S.O.: 'Safety in Outdoor Pursuits', (H.M.S.O.).
Herzog, M.: 'Anapurna'.
Hunt, J.: 'The ascent of Everest', (Hodder and Stoughton).
La Chapelle, E. R.: 'The ABC of Avalanche Safety', (available Glenmore Lodge).
Meldrum and Parker: 'Outdoor Education', (Dent), 1973.

Milne, M.: 'The book of modern mountaineering', (Barker), 1968.
Moffat, G.: 'Space beneath my feet'.
Murray, W. H.: 'The story of Everest', (Dent), 1953; 'Undiscovered Scotland', (Dent), 1954; 'Mountaineering in Scotland', (Dent), 1947, (Albyn paperback).
Noyce, W.: 'South Col'; 'Men and Mountains'.
Noyce, Sutton and Young: 'Snowdon biography.'
Patey, T.: 'One man's mountains', (Gollanz), 1971.
Poucher, W. A.: 'The Lakeland Peaks', (Constable); 'The Scottish Peaks', (Constable); 'The Welsh Peaks', (Constable).
Pyatt, E. C.: 'Where to climb in the British Isles', (Faber).
Pyatt, E. C. and M. E.: 'Boys book of mountains and mountaineering', (Burke).
Seligman, G.: 'Snow structure and ski fields', O.P.
Shipton, E.: 'Upon that mountain', 1956, O.P.
Smith, J. A.: 'Mountain holidays', (Dent), 1953, O.P.
Styles, S.: 'The mountaineers weekend book', (Seeley Service).
Sutton and Noyce: 'Samson, the life and writings of Menlove Edwards', O.P.
Terray, L.: 'Conquistadors of the Useless', (Gollanz), 1957, O.P.
Ward, M.: 'The mountaineers companion', (Eyre and Spottiswoode), 1966.
Wright, J. E. B.: 'Rock climbing in Britain', (Kaye).
Whymper, E.: 'Scrambles amongst the Alps', (Murray), O.P.
Young, G. W.: 'On High Hills', (Methuen), O.P.

Natural History

Collins' New Naturalist Series: This is an outstanding and comprehensive series, some in paperback and some hard cover only. Titles include: 'Mountains and Moorlands', 'The Highlands and Islands', 'Mountain Flowers', 'Britain's Structure and Scenery' and many others.
Other series:
Collins' Pocket/Field Guides:
Blanford Colour Series:
Hamlyn, all colour, paperbacks:

Burke's Young Specialist Series:
Observer Book Series:
Forestry Commission: available from H.M.S.O.
The Oxford Book Series:

Magazines

'*Mountain Life*' (bi-monthly). The official magazine of the B.M.C. c/o The Navigators House, River Lane, Richmond, Surrey, TW10 7AG.
'*Climber and Rambler*' (monthly). Holmes, McDougall Ltd., 36 Tay Street, Perth, PH1 5TT.
'*Mountain*' (monthly). An international 'glossy' Mountain Magazines Ltd., c/o 56 Sylvester Road, London N2.

Films

A comprehensive list of films dealing with mountaineering practice may be obtained from the British Mountaineering Council, Crawford House, Precinct Centre, Booth Street East, Manchester M13 9RZ.

Guide Books, Journals

Most mountain areas in the U.K. are covered by general guides, such as those produced by the Scottish Mountaineering Club for the various Scottish regions. Rock climbing guides are also published by the climbing clubs; in the Lake District by the Fell and Rock, in North Wales by the Climbers Club and in Scotland by the Scottish Mountaineering Club. Climbing clubs throughout the country produce journals which may be on sale to the public.

Join a Club

It is always worthwhile joining a mountaineering club.
  For English, Welsh, and N. Irish clubs contact: The Secretary, British Mountaineering Council, Crawford House, Precinct Centre, Booth Street East, Manchester M13 9RZ.
  For Scottish clubs contact: The Secretary, Mountaineering Council for Scotland, 11 Kirklee Quadrant, Glasgow, G12 0TS.

Appendix D: Sample theory papers

Appendix D1

Mountain Leadership Training Board for England and Wales: Examples of Written Questions for Final Assessment

■ Outline the main principles one should adopt in clothing oneself for a mountain walk.

■ Discuss points you would look for when buying a mountaineering boot.

■ Explain the factors you would consider and observe when planning a mountain walk for a party of school children.

■ State what effects weather and altitude can have upon mountain walkers.

■ Explain what considerations the leader of a mountain walk should observe before, during and after an expedition.

■ State what one should remember when scrambling and walking in mountain terrain.

■ Discuss what you consider to be basic essentials of rucksack designs and manufacture.

■ State the factors you would look for in choosing a camp site.

■ What points would you include in a message for a mountain rescue?

■ What equipment would be required for a rescue of a climber with an injured leg situated halfway up a mountain crag?

■ State two conditions when morphine must not be administered to an injured person.

■ How would you keep a person suffering from exposure as comfortable as possible while waiting for the rescue team?

■ Give your impressions concerning solo mountaineering.

■ What do you think are the usual reasons for the majority of mountain accidents?

■ What are the safety factors involved in planning a mountain walk?

■ Discuss the symptoms, effects and treatment of exposure.

■ Describe a sequence of actions if a member of your party of 10 boys sprains an ankle on one of the Snowdon ridges.

■ What considerations are involved in moving and keeping a party together on a mountain walk and scramble?

■ What essential pieces of equipment would you take when leading a party of boys on a mountain walk in winter for optimum safety and comfort?

■ Assuming a direct line on flat ground how many kilometres distance are there between the Mountain Rescue post in grid square 6655 and the western edge of the lake in square 6055?

■ In grid square 7352 there are many conventional signs (or symbols). Enumerate them, describing very briefly what each represents (e.g. M.S. = milestone).

■ Give a six-figure grid reference for your position if you can see Moel Hebog (5646) on a forward magnetic bearing of 298° and Snowdon (6054) on a forward magnetic bearing of 18°.

■ Assuming a direct line, what magnetic bearing would you march on doing a journey from the mountain summit in grid square 7162 to the crossroads in 7258?

■ Discuss the various factors which a group leader would need to take into account in assessing the time required for a mountain journey.

■ Define a convex slope and give an example from your map. Do you consider that such slopes are good or bad routes down a mountain? Give reasons.

■ What are the special problems of navigation in mist and how would you attempt to solve them?

■ Plan a high level mountain walk including magnetic bearings of escape routes, from Beddgelert 591482 to Betws-Garmon 536576.

Appendix D2

Scottish Mountain Leadership Training Board Summer Certificate – Assessment: Map and Compass Theory: Written Examination – Typical Questions

1 Give a six-figure map reference for:
(*a*) The summit of Ben Macdhui.....................
(*b*) The Shelter Stone.....................
(*c*) Glenmore Lodge ....

2 Identify the following map references:
(*a*) 994093 ....
(*b*) 045057 ....
(*c*) 927078 ....

3 How high above sea level are the following?
(*a*) Lochan Uaine 025986.....................
(*b*) Lochan Uaine 959980.....................
(*c*) Lochan Uaine 001105.....................

4 What is the magnetic bearing from:
(*a*) Airgiod-Meall 965067 to 950065.....................
(*b*) 906046 to 911057? ....

5 Uniform Slope: Saddle: High Plateau: Convex Slope: Crag and Coire: Arete: Spur: Re-entrant.
Which of the above best describe the main topographical feature in the grid squares below?
0411 ....
9898 ....
9811 ....
0308 ....
9499 ....
9904 ....
9597 ....
9696 ....

6 How would you find North with the aid of a watch on a bright sunny day?

7 Write in few lines on magnetic variation and how it alters from place to place and year to year.

8 Describe in detail a walk along the marked footpath from 034992 to 003017.

9 You have a reasonably fit party of 14-year-olds carrying full camping kit. How long would you expect the journey to take from the Army Ski Hut 950065 to Corrour 981959 via the Lairig Ghru? ....

10 Your magnetic bearing to Derry Cairngorm 017981 is 333° and to Carn a Mhaim 998950 is 241°. Where are you?.....................
....

11 Fill in Section A of a route card for a journey from Cairntoul 963973 to Braeriach 943999.

Appendix D3

Scottish Mountain Leadership Certificate (Summer): Mountain Safety

1 Write not more than 50 words on each of the following:
Wind chill
Naismith's rule
Frostbite
Morphia
Shivering

2 (*a*) List five symptoms of exposure.
(*b*) How would you treat a case of exposure *in the field* assuming you were carrying normal camping gear?
(*c*) What is the treatment of preference back at base and note any exceptions?

3 You are in charge of a small party of 14-year-old schoolchildren who are well equipped and have already had a little mountain walking experience. The intention is a July ascent of a 3000 ft. mountain in the West Highlands.
(*a*) The mountain is unknown to you, what enquiries would you make beforehand?
(*b*) What points concerning mountain safety and discipline would you revise immediately prior to departure?
(*c*) What special equipment would you carry to meet your responsibilities as party leader?

4 What formation is adopted by a party on a steep scree slope? Why?

5 What type of light is filtered by good sunglasses?

6 You see a distress signal. What is the first thing you do?

7 State two limitations of vibram-soled boots.

8 What action would you take if you were caught in an electric storm on a ridge?

9 What do these initials stand for: M.R.C. of S., M.C.S., S.M.C.?

10 What is the most effective treatment for blisters?

11 When does the deer stalking season start in Scotland?

12 You should take off your belay when you hear this call, 'Taking in'. True or False?

Appendix D4

Weather

Forecast Weather Map: Midday, Middle of February (see fig. A)

Occluded front lying across S.W. Great Britain moving N.E. at 20 knots.

Question 1

(*a*) What cloud would you expect over Glenmore at midday?

(*b*) What would be strength and direction of wind on Cairngorm Plateau at midday?

(*c*) What direction will the wind be after the front goes through the area?

(*d*) What will the weather be after the front passes and why?

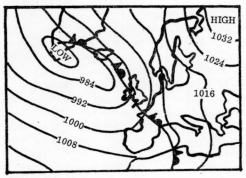

Fig. A

Question 2

What are the air masses that affect this country in Winter and where do they originate? Draw rough sketch.

Question 3

How many m.p.h. is a wind of Force 6 on the Beaufort Scale?

What sort of effect does a wind of that force have on trees?

What does this symbol mean on a weather map?

What is meant by the term, 'lapse rate'?

What is the lapse rate for saturated air?

What type of cloud heralds the approach of a depression - Cumulus, Cirro-stratus, Cumulonimbus, altocumulus, lenticular alto-cumulus?

What type of weather do you associate with a Polar continental airstream?

A katabatic wind is one which flows off high ground in the evening. True or false?

An anemometer is an instrument used for measuring: (*a*) temperature; (*b*) humidity; (*c*) wind speed; (*d*) sunshine.

Fog crystal builds up away from the wind. True or False?

If you stand with your back to the wind, which side is low pressure on?

Appendix D5

Expedition Planning –'A'

You may be asked to produce a plan for your own three-day expedition or, as in this example, for a hypothetical party of young people in your care.

You are planning a three-day expedition (two nights) to include en route the four 4000 ft. peaks of the Cairngorms. There are three members of the party, all have a reasonable amount of hill walking experience on Scottish hills in summer, but have limited rock climbing experience. Knowledge of snow conditions is limited to that acquired by reading books and pamphlets concerned with Mountain Safety. The weather forecast is good, burns are reported to be running at normal levels, though there is a light covering of snow on high ground. High camps are planned but it is not essential that full camping kit is carried throughout the three days.

1 Plan the route giving full details of each day's journey, distances involved, estimated times to be taken, camp sites and magnetic bearings where they are likely to prove useful in cloudy conditions.

2 Give a bad weather alternative for the second and third day, should the object of the trip – the four tops – have to be abandoned at noon on the second day through gale force winds. Answers to Questions 1 and 2 can either be written out in full or tabulated.

3 Give a full list of personal equipment to be worn and carried by each individual.

4 A list of equipment to be shared between the group.

5 A list of food to be taken for the three days with approximate quantities and suggested menu. Elaborate meals are not contemplated but a certain variety is desirable.

Expedition Planning – 'B'

6 Refer to your route plan for *good conditions* in Question 1. A severe thunderstorm between

8.30 a.m. and 9.30 a.m. on the third day causes burns to rise rapidly. What alteration are you likely to have to make to your route – if any?

7 You are asked to advise on the purchase of equipment for expedition use on Scottish Hills. You are assured that it will only be used between May and September. The purchaser is working to a budget and wants to get as much equipment as possible, but is conscious of the fact that it is useless to buy equipment that will not provide comfort and safety. Catalogues are supplied to assist you, though you need not restrict your choice to their contents. Suggest possible best buys of the following:

Sleeping bag
Walking boots
Rucksack
Tent – to hold three 15-year-olds.

Appendix E

Personal Equipment, including Clothing

NOTES

■ It is the Leader's responsibility to see that his party is adequately clothed and equipped.

■ See that individual loads do not exceed one-third of the body weight of the individual and in no case more than 30 lbs.

■ The delineation between LOW and HIGH level is taken to be approximately 1500 ft. above sea level.

■ Clothes not worn must be carried in the pack. A spare set of clothing must also be carried in a polythene bag and used only for night wear.

■ Ideally each member of a party should carry a personal map, compass, watch and whistle plus a torch in winter.

Summer

Low Level Walk	Low Level Camp	High Level Walk	High Level Camp
Day rations	Day rations	Map	Map
Whistle	Whistle	Day rations	Day rations
Boots	Rucksack	Compass	Compass
Stockings	Boots	Watch	Watch
Trousers	2 Stockings	Whistle	Whistle
Shirt	Plimsolls	Boots	Rucksack
Sweater	2 Trousers	Stockings	Boots
Anorak	2 Shirts	Trousers	2 Stockings
*Overanorak	2 Sweaters	Shirt	Plimsolls
First aid	Anorak	2 Sweaters	2 Trousers
	Overanorak	Anorak	2 Shirts
	First aid	*Overanorak	2 Sweaters
	Toilet requisites	*Gloves	Anorak
	Sleeping bag plus inner	First aid	Overanorak
	K.F.S.P. mug	Large polythene	Gloves
	Polythene bag	survival bag	First aid
			Toilet requisites
			Sleeping bag plus inner
			K.F.S.P. mug
			Polythene bags

(*Optional equipment depending on conditions and aim of expedition.)

Winter

Low Level Walk	Low Level Camp	High Level Walk	High Level Camp
Day rations	Day rations	Map	Map
Whistle	Whistle	Compass	Compass
Boots	Boots	Watch	Watch
Stockings	Rucksack	Whistle	Whistle
Trousers	2 Stockings	Torch	Torch
Underclothes	Plimsolls	Day rations	Day rations
Shirt	2 Trousers	Boots	Rucksack
2 Sweaters	2 Underclothes	2 Stockings	Boots
Anorak	2 Shirts	Trousers	2 Stockings
Overanorak	2 Sweaters	Overtrousers	Plimsolls
*Balaclava	Anorak	Underclothes	2 Trousers
Gloves	Overanorak	Shirt	Overtrousers
*Overmitts	Balaclava	2 Sweaters	2 Underclothes
*Light scarf	Gloves	Anorak	2 Shirts
First aid	*Overmitts	Overanorak	2/3 Sweaters
	*Light scarf	Balaclava	Anorak
	First aid	Gloves	Overanorak
	Toilet requisites	Overmitts	Balaclava
	2 Sleeping bags	Light scarf	Gloves
	plus inner	Ice axe	Overmitts
	K.F.S.P. mug	Goggles	Light scarf
	Polythene bag	Crampons	Ice axe
		First aid	Goggles
		Large polythene bag	*Crampons
			First aid
			Toilet requisites
			2 Sleeping bags
			plus inner
			K.F.S.P. mug
			Polythene bag

Communal Equipment: Shared

Summer

Low Level Walk	Low Level Camp	High Level Walk	High Level Camp
Map 1:2	*Torch 1:2	Rucksack 1:3	Mt. tent
Compass 1:2	Map 1:2		Groundsheet
Watch 1:2	Compass 1:2		Flysheet
Rucksack 1:4	Watch 1:2		Stove
	Groundsheet		Fuel and bottles
	Flysheet		Billies
	Stove		Rations
	Fuel and bottles		Water bag

*(Optional equipment depending on conditions and aim of expedition.)

Summer contd.

Low Level Walk	Low Level Camp	High Level Walk	High Level Camp
	Billies		Tin opener
	Rations		Matches
	Water bag		Brillo pads
	Tin opener		Toilet paper
	Matches		Shovel
	Brillo pads		
	Toilet paper		
	Shovel		
	Tent		

Winter

Low Level Walk	Low Level Camp	High Level Walk	High Level Camp
Rucksack 1:4	Torch 1:2	Rucksack 1:3	Mt. tent
Compass 1:2	Compass 1:2	Thermos flask	Groundsheet
Whistle 1:4	Whistle 1:4		Flysheet
Torch 1:4	Groundsheet		Stove
	Flysheet		Fuel and bottles
	Stove		Billies
	Fuel and bottles		Rations
	Billies		Water bag
	Rations		Tin opener
	Water bag		Matches
	Tin opener		Brillo pads
	Matches		Toilet paper
	Brillo pads		Shovel
	Toilet paper		
	Shovel		
	Tent		

Additional Equipment for Leader

Summer

Low Level Walk	Low Level Camp	High Level Walk	High Level Camp
First aid kit	First aid kit	120 ft. (9 mm) nylon	120 ft. (9 mm) nylon
		First aid kit	First aid kit
		Large polythene bag	Large polythene bag
		Sleeping bag	
		Emergency ration	

Winter

Low Level Walk	Low Level Camp	High Level Walk	High Level Camp
First aid kit	First aid kit	120 ft. (9 mm) nylon	120 ft. (9 mm) nylon
		First aid kit	First aid kit
		Red flare	Red flare
		Emergency ration	Emergency ration
		Sleeping bag	Large polythene bag

Winter contd.

Low Level Walk	Low Level Camp	High Level Walk	High Level Camp
		Torch batteries (extra) Large bivouac tent	Torch batteries (extra)

Appendix F

First Aid Kit

It is emphasised that the list of items given below is a suggested first aid kit to be carried by the leader of a party of up to 10 people walking or climbing on the mountains of the United Kingdom and absent from medical services for a period of less than 3 days. A first aid kit is a very personal thing and on inquiry found to contain as varied items as a ladies handbag. As with expedition rations, it is quite impossible to produce a pack which will satisfy everybody. However, most people would agree with the general principles on which this list of items has been based. These are:

1. It should be simple and avoid offering alternative treatments.
2. It should contain readily available and reasonably cheap items.
3. It should be light in weight and small in bulk.
4. As far as possible single items should be able to be used for a number of functions.
5. It should be effective and comprehensive within the above limitations.

I am greatly indebted to Dr Peter Steele and Dr Neil Macdonald for their advice and comments on the contents of this kit.

Item	No.	Use	carried by individual
Bandaid Strip 2½″ × 12″	1	quick cover for cuts and grazes.	
Anchor Dressings	4	wound closure in place of stitches, finger dressings, awkward places	2
Zinc Oxide Plaster 1″ × 5m	1	holding gauze dressings in place to secure bandages	1
Bandages 4″ Crepe	2	elasticity for support/absorbent for bleeding	1
Triangular (compressed)	1	arm sling/head bandage etc.	
Dressings Melolin gauze squares			
4″ × 4″	2	non-stick absorbent cover	1
2″ × 2″	2		
plain gauze squares 4″ × 4″	1		
Wound dressing (compressed gauze)	1	to stop bleeding in large wound	1
Antiseptic, sachet or cream	2	for dirty wounds	
Scissors, Blunt/sharp	1		
Forceps, oblique end	1	for splinters	
Scalpel blade	1		
Safety pin (nappy)	1		
Luggage label Pencil (wax and plain)	4	for written messages	1
Aspirin/Paracetamol	24	for pain	
Calamine Cream	1	for sunburn/itching	
Insect repellant	1	mosquitos/midges etc.	
Suncream, lip salve	1	optional – should filter U.V.	Op.
Wintergreen cream	1	optional – aching muscles, sprains	Op.

The Winter Certificate

II The Winter Certificate Syllabus

The Mountain Leadership Certificate (Winter) provides training in the very exacting skills required for taking parties on to mountains under winter conditions. It is intended primarily for candidates for the Instructors' Certificates, for whom it forms an essential part of the training requirements, but it is also open to those who, having gained the Mountain Leadership Certificate (Summer), seek this particular qualification only.

To lead a party into the Scottish mountains in winter conditions is a serious undertaking. Demands are made on the leader which are far in excess of his normal responsibilities in summer. For this reason, only competent all-round mountaineers with experience of winter climbing will be likely to satisfy Assessment requirements.

Courses at Mountain Centres, valuable though they are, require to be supplemented by personal experience over a considerable period. Quite stringent requirements are, therefore, laid down in this Syllabus.

The Winter Certificate Scheme is administered solely by the Scottish Mountain Leadership Training Board.

Requirements

Candidates who apply for Assessment must hold the Mountain Leadership Certificate (Summer).

This requirement does not apply absolutely to registered candidates for the Mountaineering Instructors' Certificate Schemes for which there are special conditions.

All candidates, however, must hold a currently valid Adult Certificate in First Aid (of the British Red Cross Society, St. Andrew's/St. John's Ambulance Associations or the Armed Services First Aid Certificate), as required for the Summer Certificate, which must be presented at Assessment.

The scheme of training, experience and Assessment will be conducted on the same lines as those instituted for the Summer Certificate.

The following must be completed to the satisfaction of the Board:

A Basic Training Course lasting at least one week or a planned seies of at least four weekends at a Centre approved by the Board for the specific purpose of staging Basic Training for the Winter Certificate. A weekend will consist of two full days' activity.

Candidates are required to gain practical experience of winter climbing over a minimum period of two seasons, one of these in Scotland or in a major mountain range abroad, e.g. Alps, and to have experience of differing types of snow conditions.

Candidates are required to present a detailed record of expeditions and experience in an official personal Log Book to the Director at the commencement of the week of assessment.

Candidates may find it to their advantage to attend appropriate courses; Snow and Ice Climbing, Winter Survival, Mountain Rescue, etc. Details of such courses available in Scotland may be obtained from the Secretary.

A residential period of Assessment, lasting at least one week, at a centre approved by the Board. (At present, Glenmore Lodge is the only centre so approved.)

Textbooks

All candidates are required to be conversant with 'Mountain Leadership' the official handbook of the Mountain Leadership Training Boards; 'Safety on Mountains'; 'Mountain and Cave Rescue'.

These publications are available from the following sources:

The Scottish Sports Council, 1 St. Colme Street, Edinburgh EH3 6AA.

The Sports Council, 49 Malone Road, Belfast BT9 6RZ.

The British Mountaineering Council, Crawford House, Precinct Centre, Booth Street East, Manchester M13 9RZ.

Syllabus

For Assessment purposes, candidates will be required to be familiar with the theory and practice of the following:

1 Carrying the ice axe.
2 Kicking steps up and down in snow.
3 Use of the axe; walking, step cutting up and down, belaying, glissading, probing.
4 Braking, in self-arrest technique.
5 Holding a fall on steep snow from above and from below.
6 Step cutting on ice, with and without crampons.
7 Cramponing up and down, and traversing.
8 Belaying on ice – use of pitons and screws.
9 Surmounting a cornice.
10 Moving together.
11 Winter climbing at Grade I standard.
12 Special equipment, individual and group, necessary for winter mountaineering.
13 Winter Campcraft.
14 Construction of snow holes and emergency shelter.
15 Knowledge of the causes, symptoms and treatment of exposure and frostbite.
16 A knowledge of the development of weather systems in winter.
17 A basic knowledge of the process of firnification and evaluation of avalanche risk.
18 Winter search and evacuation techniques, including the searching of avalanche tips.
19 A sound knowledge of the planning of winter expeditions and the special responsibilities of the party leader.

Exemptions

Experienced mountaineers may consider approaching the Board with a view to exemption from the initial training requirements in order that they may proceed more directly to assessment. Details and conditions for such exemption will be made available on application to the Secretary, S.M.L.T.B.

Assessment

Candidates will be assessed on the basis of ability to lead others in winter conditions as well as their personal competence in the various skills.

The Board will appoint a Director of Assessment to whom shall be delegated the responsibility for making all necessary arrangements.

Subsequent to Assessment of candidates, the Director of Assessment will make recommendations to the Board regarding the award of Certificates.

All enquiries should be addressed to: The Secretary, Scottish Mountain Leadership Training Board, Scottish Sports Council, St. Colme Street, Edinburgh EH3 6AA. (Tel. 031-225 8411).
The Secretary, Mountain Leadership Training Board, Crawford House, Precinct Centre, Booth Street East, Manchester M13 9RZ.
The Secretary, Northern Ireland Mountain Leadership Training Board, The Sports Council, 49 Malone Road, Belfast, BT9 6RZ. (Tel. 0232 66 9519).

13 Snow and ice climbing

The lesson plans which follow are not intended to be crammed into one or two days, but rather they should be spread out over the whole period of training. The emphasis throughout should be on basic techniques and the importance of practising braking and belaying cannot be overstressed. Braking is the one vital skill which must be taught to the members of any party going on to the hills with ice axes in winter conditions. It should be taught and practised thoroughly by all on the first suitable snow slope irrespective of their objective for that particular day. The margin of error on snow and ice is small indeed and only absolute familiarity with basic techniques will bring the personal confidence that is necessary to lead a party in complete safety.

During the period of training advantage must be taken of conditions as they arise and any programme must be flexible enough to allow for this. For example there would be little point in teaching braking in snow which was sufficiently soft and wet to make it impossible to pick up any speed. Similarly, crampon technique should be taught on firm snow and not on wet slush or 'balling' snow where they could in fact be a positive danger. If snow conditions are unsuitable for cramponing they may be just right for something else, such as instruction in belaying with 'dead men'.

Choice of terrain is an equally important factor in training and especially in the initial period when students are encouraged to 'fall off' in order to practise braking and holding techniques. A clear run out at the bottom of the practice slope where they can come to rest without harm is essential. Though the occasional rock can be padded with rucksacks and clothing, slopes with protruding rocks should be avoided, as should those which give on to steep scree. If, however, these are the only slopes available the students must be safeguarded by other methods. This means that the rope must be introduced earlier than it otherwise would and belaying and holding techniques taught from the very first. In this way further practice may be suitably safeguarded.

The angle of the slope, too, is important. If more advanced techniques suitable for high angle snow or ice are taught on easy ground, it can give the student a completely false idea of the purpose and effectiveness of that particular skill. The ideal slope is a concave one on which a progression can easily be followed from gentle to steep ground.

Winter climbing offers great scope for the perfection of individual style. Such variations are to be encouraged and improved upon as perfectly natural expressions of a built-in 'way of moving'. There is, however, no room for slipshod rope handling and belaying or for the use of out-dated and insecure techniques. The psychological belay is seen far too often on winter climbs. No belay should be arranged that could not with confidence be put to the test. Practice is the essence of winter training;

practice in falling off and braking the fall; practice in holding a fall; practice in abseiling from snow bollards and so on. It is often difficult to say that one technique is better than another especially since they may both be good, but for different snow conditions. Test and compare them in as many situations as possible. If, for example, it is belaying techniques which are being considered they should be set up and tested to destruction. In this way students will see and feel for themselves the relative merits of the different systems.

The training sessions provide the background on which a candidate for the Certificate can build his experience. They can never be more than this but they do provide a unique opportunity for concentrated learning. For this reason ascents of actual routes should be kept to a maximum of one or two, with their function more to show how the various skills learned are employed on a climb rather than to introduce and practise any new techniques. Candidates are expected to be able to lead up to Grade I when they present themselves for Assessment. The following table gives a summary of what is involved in the various grades of climb:

GRADE I: Straightforward, average angled snow gullies, generally showing no pitches under adequate snow cover. They may, however, present cornice difficulty or have dangerous outruns in the event of a fall.

GRADE II: Pitches encountered in gullies, or gullies with high-angle and difficult cornice exits. The easier buttresses which under snow present more continuous difficulty.

GRADE III: Serious climbs which should only be undertaken by parties with good experience.

GRADE IV: Routes of sustained difficulty or climbs of the highest standard which are too short to be described as Grade V.

GRADE V: Routes which give major expeditions and are only to be climbed when conditions are favourable.

Snow and ice climbing lesson plan

Indoor Session

Subject	Content	Notes
EQUIPMENT	Rope. Slings and tapes. Karabiners.	Hawser and kernmantel lay. Care of rope, slings, and karabiners. Screw gate for waist line, or harness, or tie directly to waist.
	Boots.	Warmth – kicking steps – taking crampons.
	Gaiters.	
	Axe.	Wood, glass fibre or metal shaft. Selection of quality wood shaft. Length for walking and for climbing. Design of head, including angle of pick. Wrist slings for novices. Carrying holster.

Fig. 46: The ice axe

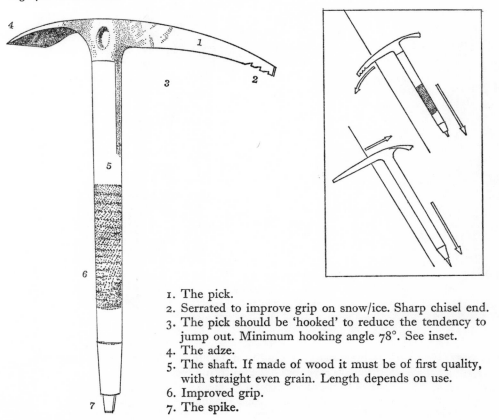

1. The pick.
2. Serrated to improve grip on snow/ice. Sharp chisel end.
3. The pick should be 'hooked' to reduce the tendency to jump out. Minimum hooking angle 78°. See inset.
4. The adze.
5. The shaft. If made of wood it must be of first quality, with straight even grain. Length depends on use.
6. Improved grip.
7. The spike.

Subject	Content	Notes
	Crampons.	Fixed and adjustable – spring fit – 10 or 12 points – straps – stress great care in use. – Sharpening.

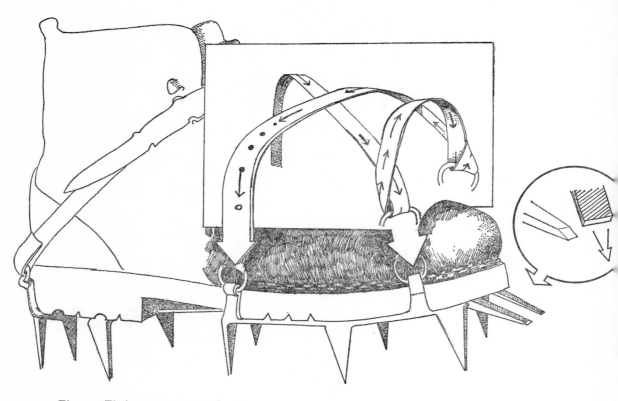

Fig. 47: Fitting crampons to boots

	Dagger. Hammer-axe. Pitons. Hammer. Screws. Gloves. Clothing. Goggles.	
KNOTS	Figure of eight on the bight to karabiner on hemp waist line or harness. Prussik knot Clove hitch. Tape knot.	
BELAYS	Indirect belay to 'dead man' taking the active rope round the waist. Indirect belay to metal shafted axe or snow stake. Snow / ice bollard. Ice pitons and screws. Rock belays.	This is the basic method.

Subject	Content	Notes
CLIMBING CALLS	'Taking in' – '*That's me*' – 'Climb when you're ready' – '*Climbing*' – 'O.K.'	

Outdoor Sessions

Terrain: Slope of firm snow starting from the flat or nearly so and gradually steepening to an angle of between 30° and 45°. The flat or gently sloping run out and the slope itself must be free of protruding rocks or other obstructions.

Subject	Content	Notes
CARRYING THE AXE	In sack. Walking up, down and across gentle terrain.	Do not use as walking stick on stony ground. Axe should be held with the pick pointing aft and the adze forward in whichever hand is the uphill one. Thus the axe is already held in the position from which it is easiest to attain a self-arrest position.
KICKING STEPS	Up gentle slope.	Position of axe – two points of contact.
	Down gentle slope.	Stress balanced position – no sitting back – axe in braking position.
	Up steep slope.	Double steps in soft snow.
	Down steep slope.	Facing in using toes – axe or pick thrust into snow.
	Traversing up and down.	Use heels as much as possible – spike of axe in snow.
BRAKING	Pick brake facing slope – increase distance and speed of slide.	One hand on axe head, other near spike – adze close to shoulder – apply gradual pressure with body weight and chest across shaft. Keep legs apart for stability. Most people brake with their right hand on the axe-head. It is better to concentrate on this, than to try to teach a left handed brake as well.
	On back facing out. Head first facing slope. Head first facing out. Tumbling fall.	The first action in any head-down or tumbling fall is to get into a head-uphill position in which conventional self-arrest technique can be used. If your back is against the slope, always roll to the same side as the hand that is holding the axe head. If you roll the other way, the spike is likely to dig into the slope and throw you outward.

Subject	Content	Notes

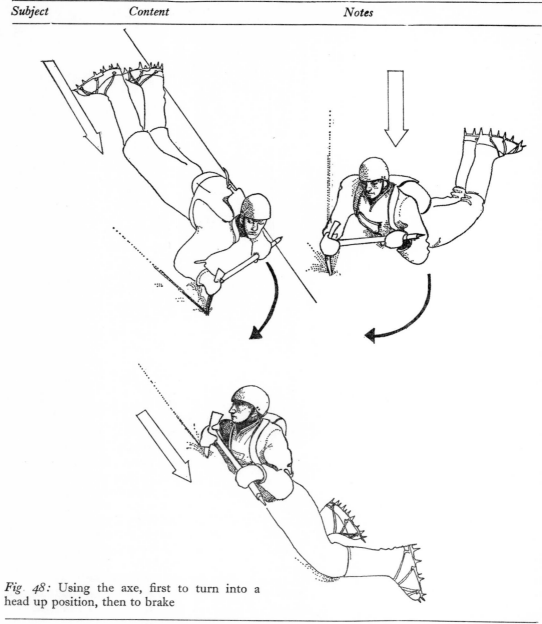

Fig. 48: Using the axe, first to turn into a head up position, then to brake

STEP CUTTING	Diagonally up. Diagonally down. Straight up. Straight down.	No crampons – attention to rhythm, shape and spacing of steps – remember you may have to retreat down them – always cut into the hole made by first stroke – in slab snow cut ╱ with pick and chop out by completing ╱ with adze.

Subject	Content	Notes
THE ROPE	Tying on, using figure of eight on the bight, to screwgate krab on hemp waist line.	
BELAYING	Indirect belay to 'dead man'. Practise holding second.	See separate notes on Belaying. Active rope round waist. Wear gloves. Stress careful positioning of 'dead man' and relation to stance. Concentrate on gradual increase of braking effect.
	Indirect belay to metal shafted axe or snow stake.	Clove hitch on shaft against snow surface.
	Indirect belay to snow bollard.	Compare effectiveness of the different methods.
HOLDING A FALL	Second falls (without crampons).	Gradually increase length of fall up to 15 ft. or so.
	Leader falls (without crampons)	Continue practise until holding falls of up to 40 ft. – alter the angles.
CLIMBING	Grade I climb in pitches leading through.	Without crampons – use standard system of climbing calls. Stances determined by position of best
	Same in descent.	belays and not by length of rope.

Terrain: As for previous session, but with steeper section for teaching more advanced crampon techniques (e.g. front point cramponing) and abseiling. The snow must be hard.

CRAMPONING	Ascending traverse.	Stress all points in, with toes pointing down at an angle. Use of axe with progressive *increase in slope*.
	Descending traverse.	Turn facing out. *Practise with steps on steep slopes*.
	Straight descent.	Toes pointing down and body arched outwards. Axe held in braking position with, or without, support *from the spike*.
FRONT POINT CRAMPONING	Up and down.	Using two axes, or axe and dagger. Boots should be kept horizontal. Do not kick front *points in too hard*.
BRAKING	Short slides with crampons.	*Great care necessary*. Keep the feet off the snow.
GLISSADING	Don't.	Very common cause of winter accidents – explain why.
CLIMBING	Grade I – II climb using crampons.	

Subject	Content	Notes

Terrain: Ice bulges often found away from crag in more broken terrain. The type of ground that in summer consists of short wet walls and slabs separated by irregular terraces. More serious ice climbing should only be undertaken after experience has been gained on safer ground. In any case a high standard of ice climbing is not required for the Winter Certificate.

Subject	Content	Notes
ICE	Note the varying quality.	This may vary from day to day according to temperature and prevailing conditions.
CRAMPONING	Up and down and traverse on easy angled ice.	With crampons. Practise without using support from axe or dagger.
STEP-CUTTING	As above on progressively steeper ice.	Dual purpose steps or handholds cut with pronounced lip.
BELAYING	Rock belays and pitons in rock. Ice pitons and screws.	Most effective method. Try variety of types and test to find type best suited for particular kind of ice.
	Ice bollard.	A most effective belay if fashioned correctly. Practise and test.
ABSEILING	Classic and sit-sling method from piton, 'dead man' or ice bollard. Easy diagonal abseiling.	A safety rope must be used at all times. With crampons.
CLIMBING	Grade II climb with straightforward ice pitch and cornice.	
CORNICES	Chopping through.	Second belayed well to one side – danger of wind slab on scarp face below cornice.
	Tunnelling.	Use hand on adze as a scraper. Snow saw if carried makes short work of this. More advanced technique involving artificial climbing or combined tactics are not required.

14 Belaying on snow and ice

Belaying on snow is considered to be one of the more important skills which the Winter Mountain Leader must become familiar with. Unfortunately, current literature on the subject advocates traditional techniques which are based on false premises and which do not stand up to critical examination and practical tests. For these reasons this subject receives rather fuller treatment than it otherwise would in the hope that mountaineers will be encouraged to take a more realistic view of security on snow and ice.

Ice axes were not designed with belaying in mind. Primarily they were, and are, instruments for cutting steps in snow and ice. Other functions have arisen later out of necessity, without too much regard being paid to suitability for this multipurpose role. Traditional methods of belaying place a completely unjustified reliance on the strength of the axe shaft, often without sparing a thought for the material in which it is embedded. Metal shafted axes are the only ones which can be used for this purpose with any degree of confidence, but the strongest shaft in the world is useless if the snow itself is going to fracture under the expected loading. Accident records show quite clearly that very often when a leader falls off on a winter climb he pulls the remainder of the party off with him. No doubt belaying on snow or ice can never match the security available on rock, but at the same time it could be a great deal safer than it is. In this chapter techniques are outlined and related to varying kinds of snow.

Two initial hurdles must be overcome. The first is that mountaineers tend to adopt a particular technique and use it regardless of all other factors. Many techniques are available, each one suited to particular snow conditions. The leader must be aware of these different conditions and adapt his methods accordingly.

The second point is that all these techniques demand very careful application. A badly placed axe, an inadequate stance, a rope in the wrong place, all can lead to disaster.

Types of belay. The shaded areas indicate suitable techniques for various conditions of snow

	Conventional axe belay	Indirect belay to 'dead man' with waist belay	Indirect belay to metal shafted axe or snow stake	Bollard	Ice screws	Rock belay
Powder snow	—	▪	—	—	—	▪
Wet snow (porridge)	—	▪	—	—	—	▪
Wind consolidated snow (slab)	—	▪	—	—	—	▪
Old snow (soft)	—	▪	—	—	—	▪
Old snow (hard)	—	▪	▪	▪	—	▪
Ice	—	—	—	▪	▪	▪

Belaying techniques must be practised

The table above shows the types of belay which are recommended for six different conditions of snow, assuming that the function of the belay is to provide some protection for the leader and the party as a whole. The degree of protection afforded by a conventional wooden-shafted axe is minimal and for this reason its use as an anchor is not recommended. There is little doubt that the most reliable belays are to be found on rock – on gully walls, on rock outcrops or even on rocks embedded in the ice. This is particularly true on ice climbs and every opportunity should be taken to secure the party to the rock, whether by piton or by using natural features. This is certainly one situation where the use of artificial aids should be encouraged. The chart must be read with this in mind. So, too, it is worth remembering that the snow cover is normally a layered structure and though the surface layer may be unconsolidated, there may well be a firm under-layer affording better possibilities for belaying.

Wooden-shafted Axe Belay:

This traditional method is unsafe in almost all conditions and is NOT recommended. In good, hard snow which will support the axe the leverage applied under shock loading is likely to break the shaft. Wood shafted axes in current use are not designed to stand up to this sort of strain. In snow of lesser cohesion the snow itself is the weak link; the axe pivots and pulls out.

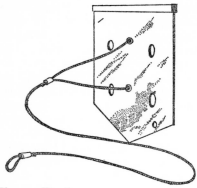

Fig. 49: Dead man

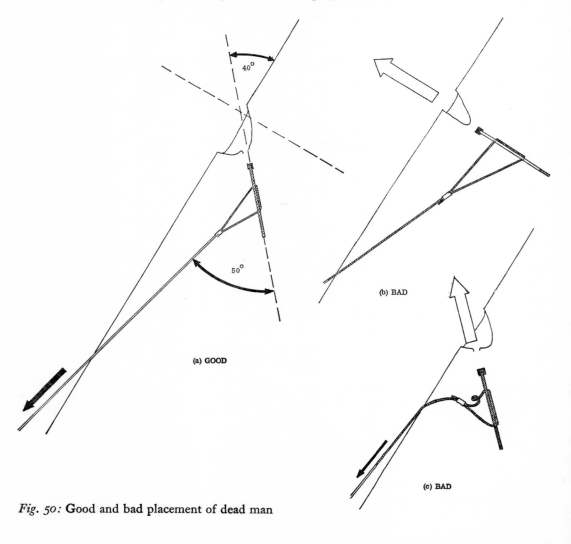

Fig. 50: Good and bad placement of dead man

Indirect Belay to 'Dead Man':

The 'dead man', shown in Fig. 49, is a spade-shaped alloy plate reinforced on one edge and with a 6 ft. wire attached centrally. The principle is that the plate is embedded in the snow in such a way that its entire surface resists movement through the snow when a load is applied to the wire. This method has the merit of working in most kinds of snow, particularly in poorly-consolidated snow, where traditional methods offer little or no security. Careful placing of the 'dead man' to avoid pulling out is absolutely vital and it must always be test-loaded before use. This also has the effect of bedding the 'dead man' in.

A slot should be cut in the snow at least 10 ft. above the stance, taking care to disturb the snow as little as possible in the immediate area. The 'dead man' is inserted at the bottom of this slot in such a way that the plane of the plate makes an angle of approximately 40° with the snow surface. A convenient way to estimate this angle is to hold the ice axe at 90° to the surface just over the slot. Bisect this angle with the plate and then tilt it back a further 5° and push it home. Most ice axes have a lip near the spike and this can be used to tap the plate into the snow to a depth of at least one foot. When the wire is pulled from below it goes through the snow like a cheese-cutter and, save on the hardest of snow or ice, will adopt the correct position, shown in Fig. 50(a). In snow/ice it may be necessary to clear out a passage for the wire to prevent it hooking, as in Fig. 50(c). In this illustration a sudden load on the wire could jerk the 'dead man' out of the snow.

The stance should be taken at least 10 ft. below the 'dead man'. This will ensure that the internal angle between the plate and the wire does not exceed 50°. Clearly, a high stance will result in a dangerous increase of this angle. The climber belays to the 'dead man' in the normal way, adopting a sitting position for maximum holding power, with the added benefit of reducing the 'dead man' angle.

Many winter climbs finish on flat ground, on a ridge, or at the edge of a plateau. It is often difficult to provide any satisfactory belay in such a situation. The 'dead man' is just as efficient buried in a horizontal position as in any other and exactly the same rules apply for placement. The stance must be well back from any cornice

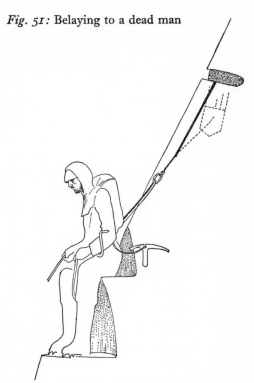

Fig. 51: Belaying to a dead man

and that means that the 'dead man' may be as much as 25 ft. – 30 ft. back from the edge. (Fig. 52).

Since the 'dead man' depends for its successful operation on the cohesion of the snow, it is particularly important that this is not disturbed in any way. Special care must be taken in slabby snow not to fracture the whole retaining mass of snow. The rule is that if the snow has good natural cohesion, e.g. old snow, wind slab, wet slab, disturb it as little as possible, but if, on the other hand, it lacks cohesion, e.g. powder snow, wet snow, then the whole area should be stamped down.

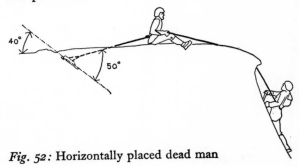

Fig. 52: Horizontally placed dead man

Indirect Belay to the Ice Axe

Metal shafted axes, either tubular or reinforced, are the only ones which can be recommended with any confidence and then only for indirect belaying on hard snow when the axe can be hammered home. In snow softer than this the snow itself becomes the weak link and will not support the axe in position.

The axe should be placed at 90° to the snow surface, then tilted back 20°–30° and driven in. On no account cut a step for the axe. A long sling should be attached to the shaft in such a way that it lies against the snow, the stance being taken at least 10 ft. below the axe. Belay as to a 'dead man' and in a sitting position.

It is perhaps worth noting that the axe itself can be used as a 'dead man' particularly in snow which can be consolidated by stamping. The rope should be attached to the shaft by a clove hitch some 3″ towards the head end from the middle and the axe should then be laid horizontally in a trough cut in the snow, with the rope coming out to the surface at right angles to the axe. The whole thing must then be well stamped in and tested. The method is not so effective as the 'dead man' and can only be recommended if one is not available. However, under the conditions described it is much superior to a conventional vertical axe belay.

Indirect Belay to Snow Stake

A snow stake is an alloy tube or piece of angle alloy, 18″ to 2 ft. long. It provides an excellent belay in hard snow in just the same way as the metal shafted axe but, of course, has the advantage that it can be hammered without fear of damage. A rough guide as to the strength of the snow is to attempt to drive the axe shaft in a single violent thrust. If you succeed in driving it in more than 1 ft. then the snow is too soft to support either an axe or a snow stake belay. The method used is identical to the axe belay.

Bollard (see Fig. 55)

This is one of the safest methods of belaying on hard snow or ice, but unfortunately a bollard takes some time to cut, especially in ice. However, at a difficult pitch or for an abseil the extra time involved may be well worth while.

The neck of the bollard should be padded to

Fig. 53: Horizontal axe belay

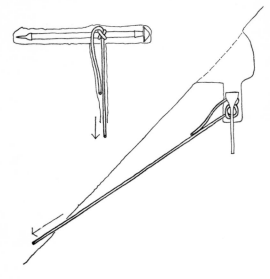

Fig. 54: Snow stakes

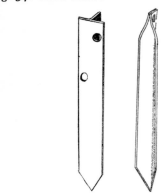

Fig. 55: Snow or ice bollard. A bollard cut in soft snow may be as much as 5 ft. across

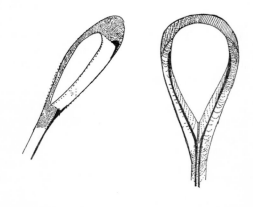

prevent cutting in and to distribute any load over as large an area as possible. The size is governed by the type of snow or ice, but generally speaking they should never be less than 15″ in diameter. Here again, it is not intended that the bollard should take the whole shock load of a fall, but that the climber should be secured to it and take the active rope round his waist in the normal way. Do not use a bollard in slabby, layered snow where the rope is liable to pull through. The groove may be warmed with the hand so that melting and refreezing reinforces the surface.

Ice Screws

In general ice screws do not make satisfactory belays, not because of any defects in design or manufacture, though undoubtedly some makes are better than others, but rather because of the inherent weakness of ice. Ice on British mountains tends to be brittle and although a screw may appear to be solidly in and will certainly support a steady load, under shock load the ice may well fracture. Ice screws and pitons therefore should always be used with caution and only as a main belay when alternative methods are not practicable.

In this event, several screws should be linked together to afford greater security. In addition to the straight blade, channel, or tubular piton, there are 2 basic types of ice screws; these are screw in – screw out and drive in – screw out. There are, of course, many variations within these broad categories and no one screw performs well in every type of ice. For this reason most climbers carry a selection, depending on the climb and the prevailing conditions.

As with rock pitons, it is important that the head of the screw lies flush with the ice. If not, it must be tied-off. For this reason screws are inserted at right angles to the surface of the ice. Any rotten ice should be cut away and a sloping step cut behind, in the good ice. The screw goes in at the back of this step, allowing sufficient room for the revolution of the head. (Fig. 56). 'Shattering' or 'dinner plating' are two fairly common mishaps when putting in ice screws. When this happens, try again.

Rock Pitons

Since it is quite normal to use rock pitons on snow and ice routes, a brief word on their use is called for. Most modern pitons are of the hard steel type and can be classified into three main groups: blades, angles and those with a Z section (leepers). Correct placement is very important, to allow for the maximum mechanical advantage and torque. The piton should be placed in the crack to about two-thirds of its length by hand and then hammered home, so that the eye is flush with the rock. If it is not, the piton should be tied-off with a short loop of tubular tape. It may also have to be tied-off if there is any possibility of the karabiner acting as a lever against the rock.

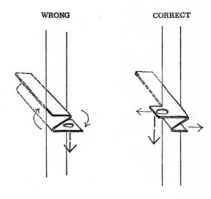

Fig. 57: (*a*) Placement of pitons. For maximum torque

NB: It follows that on a horizontal crack the piton should be placed with the eye down

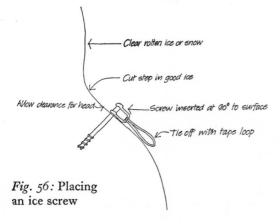

Fig. 56: Placing an ice screw

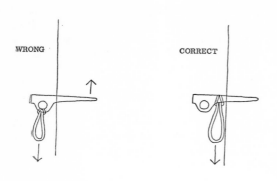

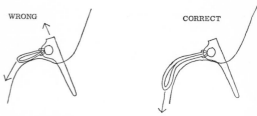

Fig. 57: (b) Placement of pitons. Tying-off

Do not overdrive pitons. Both the resistance to the hammer and the rising ring of the piton as it is struck, give an indication of when to stop.

15 Snow shelters

There are four types of snow shelters; the snow cave, the snow pit, the igloo and the soft snow mound. There are literally hundreds of variations and possible combinations of these types, each suited to particular snow and weather conditions. In Scotland the snow cave is the most reliable, since it is the only one with the structural strength to withstand sudden and devastating thaws. It is normally possible to construct some kind of snow shelter, provided there is sufficient snow. This is not likely to be found on exposed ridges or plateaux. Seek out the deeper drifts in more sheltered localities lower down. A distinction must be drawn between what can be accomplished in a matter of half an hour or so, when survival is at stake and the more luxurious shelter taking four or five hours to complete. In emergency situations they have saved many lives and they have been used extensively in polar regions and on expeditions all over the world. A well designed snow shelter affords complete protection from the wind. It is well insulated by the snow, which is a poor conductor of heat and is, therefore, quickly heated by body warmth alone. It is quiet, easily lighted and adaptable. Unfortunately, it is time consuming work. It takes approximately $1\frac{1}{2}$ hours per man sheltered, to build and for that reason it is wise to seek a suitable location well before dark.

Choice of Shelter

The choice of the type of shelter to build is dictated by the terrain and the prevailing snow conditions. Other factors to be considered are the experience of the party, the time available, the urgency for immediate shelter and the

TERRAIN	CONDITIONS OF SNOW			
	Slab	*Very Hard*	*Wet*	*Powder*
Drifts with > 30° Face	Cave	Combined Cave/Igloo	Cave	Mound
Flat Terrain No Drifts	Igloo	Combined Pit/Igloo	Snow ball Igloo	Mound
Shallow Snow	Igloo or Mound	Igloo	Snow ball Igloo	Mound

number of people that can usefully be employed in construction work. The table below suggests the types of shelter which should be attempted for various combinations of snow conditions and terrain:

Great care must be taken to construct the shelter in a safe place. The site should not be exposed to avalanche risk, not under cornices or on dangerous snow drifts. The adequacy of the tools used for construction usually depends on the degree of preparation. Fortunately, it is always possible to do something with the axe and in the right conditions even the hands can be used to make a rudimentary snow shelter. However, a broad, short handled shovel and a large toothed snow saw can make an immense difference to the job. The saw (an ordinary 18″ saw will do the trick) is a particularly useful tool and, of course, it is a good deal lighter and less bulky than a shovel.

Precautions

Certain precautions need to be taken when using snow shelters to ensure maximum safety and comfort.

■ Only dry clothing and sleeping bags will keep you warm during the night. In addition, there is always the danger of wet clothing freezing during the night, therefore every care should be taken to see that they are kept dry and the following points need to be borne in mind:

■ Digging snow is warm work. Strip off to avoid making clothes damp with sweat which may freeze later.

■ Ensure adequate ventilation at all time. See below.

■ All equipment must be brought inside.

■ Remove any wet clothing before settling in and place them in a rucksack. Do *not* leave this in the cold air trench.

■ Place boots inside a polythene bag and take them into your sleeping bag.

■ Brush off all particles of snow clinging to clothing before entering shelter. These may melt in the warm atmosphere, wetting clothing.

■ Water vapour given off during cooking may condense, wetting clothes also. If possible, avoid having liquids boiling or simmering. Increase ventilation.

■ Use a torch instead of candles, or if this is not possible, use only one candle.

■ Insulate the body from beneath as much as possible. Avoid sleeping on polythene or other slippery material. You are liable to find yourself suddenly outside the cave.

■ Take a shovel or digging implement into the shelter with you.

■ Leave a light on in the shelter if you have to leave it for any reason during the night. It may help you to find it when you come back.

Ventilation

Nearly all the recorded accidents in snow shelters have been caused by carbon monoxide (CO) Poisoning. It can not be stressed too strongly that adequate ventilation is the most important single precaution which must be taken. Normal stove burning produces little CO. However, if the flame touches a cool surface, such as a billy filled with melting snow, combustion is not completed and considerable unburnt CO will result. The danger can be reduced by avoiding direct flame contact with the billy, but increased ventilation, both at the door and above the stove, is the only safe procedure. If you get a headache after cooking it is a clear sign that the ventilation is inadequate.

In a freshly built shelter there will always be a certain amount of air movement through the walls. This will be reduced in time, as glazing takes place on the inside. In these circumstances it is quite possible for the supply of oxygen to become exhausted. This means that even if there is no burning stove or candles, additional ventilation must be provided. The door, or at least a section of it, should be left open at all times and if drifting occurs, it should be cleared out every 2 hours.

Ventilation is also necessary to prevent over heating and melting. If the external temperature is below $-10°C$ there should be no problem. At higher temperatures some dripping is inevitable and close to freezing the structure itself may be in danger of collapse. In this event the door should be kept fully open and, if the shelter has been in use for some time, the roof can be skimmed to a thickness of a few inches to increase heat loss. A ventilation hole in the roof greatly improves the through draft.

Igloo

There are many different types of igloo, each developed in its own region and specially suited to local conditions. The type described below has been developed in Scotland and is typical of the sub-arctic igloo, designed to withstand wind and weather and above all to resist for a time sudden and sometimes disastrous increases in temperature. The thin walled variety, though quicker to construct and more elegant is quite unsuited to our conditions as it requires consistently low temperatures for construction and stability.

Any consolidated snow (damp, 'snowball' snow, old snow, etc.) can be used to build an igloo, but wind packed snow is undoubtedly the best material, cutting like a soft cheese and holding its shape like a block of masonry.

Occasionally the upper layer of snow is not suitable and must be discarded so that the underlayer can be used. Poorly consolidated snow can sometimes be improved by tramping on it and then allowing it to refreeze. Wet snow can be rolled into large snow balls which can then be cut into blocks.

To build an igloo, proceed as follows:

■ Select a safe site close to a source of good building snow. The way the blocks are mined is determined by the layering, but if possible, cut the blocks with their largest surface vertical.

■ Mark out a circle, the radius of which will be dictated by the number of people to be accom-

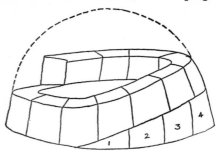

Fig. 58: Starting to build an igloo. The first blocks are trimmed to form a sloping shelf

modated. As a guide, a radius of $3\frac{1}{2}'$ should be allowed for one person, plus $\frac{1}{2}'$ for each additional person. Thus, a two man igloo will have a radius of $4'$ and a diameter of $8'$ and a four man will have a radius of $5'$ and a diameter of $10'$. Since, for stability, the igloo must approximate to a hemisphere, anything with a diameter greater than $10'$ would not be practicable.

■ The blocks should be as large as can be handled, $30''$ long, $18''$ high, with the thickness determined by the conditions: $6''$ in cold conditions, up to $15''$ if warm. They may weigh anything up to 80 lbs. The bigger the blocks the quicker the igloo will be made. Do not spend too much time trimming the blocks to the exact shape. This can be done when they are in position by running the snow saw back and forth along the joints.

Fig. 59: Igloos showing alternative entrances and wind break

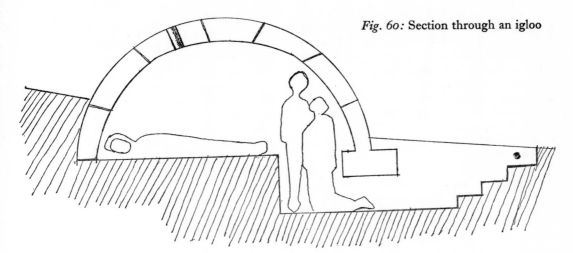

Fig. 60: Section through an igloo

■ Figs. 58–60 explain the method of construction. The builder stands inside placing the blocks in a leaning spiral and making sure that each one has three points of contact with the previous one. To do this the bottom and the side face in contact may be made slightly concave. As the igloo rises and closes in, there comes a time when the blocks have to be passed in through a temporary opening cut in the side. The final opening in the roof is sealed by passing a block through, end on, and then lowering it into position. Before closing the roof, smooth off the inside of the igloo and throw out any loose snow.

■ All the small holes in the igloo can be filled in with pieces of broken blocks and the whole structure should be covered with 6″ or more of loose snow.

■ The door should be placed at right angles to the prevailing wind. It should be approx. 2′ × 2′ and may be cut at floor level or as a trench. The latter prevents drifting, but it is time consuming to make and takes up valuable sleeping space inside. A straight forward 2′ × 2′ opening with a short tunnel, somewhat larger than the door, would seem to be the best answer. An air vent should be opened in the roof.

■ If high winds are expected a low wall should be built to windward to protect the base of the igloo against erosion.

■ If the igloo is on a slope, a level floor should be excavated first and the wall built up until it is level. A ramp can be cut and the igloo continued as before.

Furnishings and fittings can now be added the last word in luxury being a slab of clear ice inserted as a window.

Snow cave

The best locality for a snow cave is in a drift of snow with a fairly steep face, > 30°. This will ensure that there is sufficient depth of snow and that it can be easily disposed of down slope. It also means that shelter can be obtained reasonably quickly and that the snow is likely to be in good condition for cutting. It is relatively easy to make and, for Scottish conditions and emergencies, probably the most dependable type of shelter. There are many variations between the elaborate snow palace and the simple burrow which normally would have to suffice in an emergency.

The classic snow cave is constructed as follows: *See Figs. 61–63*

■ Mark the top of the projected cave with a ski stick, axe etc. Otherwise you may have unexpected company dropping in through the roof.

■ For the maximum insulation and structural stability the walls and ceiling should be at least 2′ thick.

■ Although the final entrance should be small, for ease of working it is best to make this larger and fill it in later. Dig an 8′6″ deep slot into the drift, 5′ high and 2′ wide. Blocks should be cut with a saw or shovel when possible and loose snow can be removed on a poly bag, or anorak.

■ Hot air rises therefore sleeping benches want

to be higher than the entrance. Excavate benches 2'6" wide on either side of the slot and 2' from floor level. The roof above the benches should taper from head to feet so that you are sleeping in the warm air created by your own body and not underneath it.

■ Smooth off the roof to remove dripping points and dig drainage gutters round the sleeping benches. These will allow water resulting from condensation to drain away into the cold trench.

■ Wall in the entrance completely and then cut out a hole for access at floor level. A sack or bag filled with snow makes an excellent door.

■ Make ventilation hole in roof.

Fig. 61: Section through a snow cave

Snow pit

This is not a satisfactory shelter and should only be used when no other alternatives are possible. It has much in common with a crevasse and tends to be very cold. The actual construction is simple enough except that all the material has to be thrown out of the pit. It follows much the same pattern as the Snow Cave and indeed it can be regarded as a variant of it.

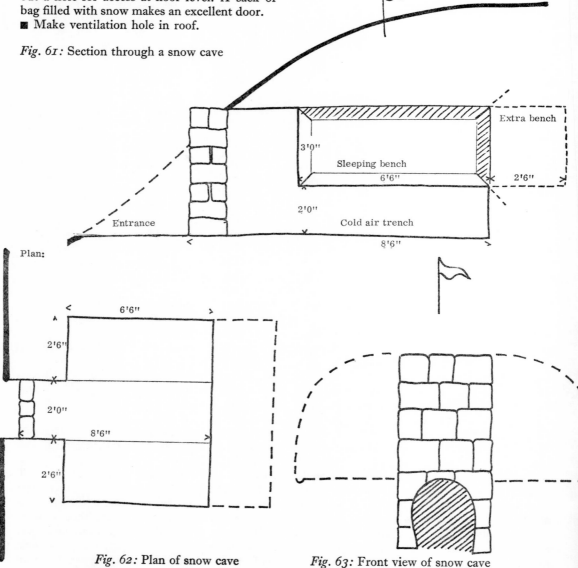

Extra bench

3'0"

Sleeping bench
6'6"

2'6"

2'0"

Entrance

Cold air trench

8'6"

Plan:

6'6"

2'6"

2'0"

8'6"

2'6"

Fig. 62: Plan of snow cave

Fig. 63: Front view of snow cave

■ Dig a pit approximately six feet long, two feet wide and six feet deep. Remove snow in blocks if possible and save these for sealing roof later.
■ Excavate sleeping chambers in the side walls of the pit. These need to be about two feet six inches high. The roof should be about two feet six inches below the surface. Each chamber needs to be deep enough to accommodate the number of persons using it; for this allow two feet six inches to three feet shelf width for each person.
■ Slope the roof of the sleeping chamber and dig drainage grooves.
■ Make ventilation holes if necessary.
■ Cover roof of pit with snow blocks, etc. See under construction of igloo.

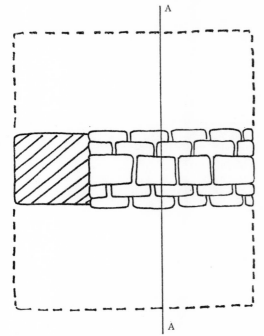

Fig. 64: Plan of snow pit

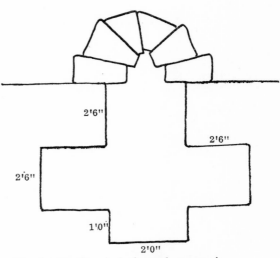

Fig. 65: Section A-A through snow pit

Soft Snow Mound

This unusual design of shelter originated in the U.S.A. where it has been successful in areas of shallow snow cover, below the timberline. When snow is disturbed it undergoes a process known as *age hardening*. It is this process which is used to consolidate shallow, loose masses of powder snow, which are later excavated to provide a shelter.
■ An axe, or ski stick is placed where the centre of the mound is to be and a circle drawn round it, of radius 2 ft. more than that required in the completed shelter. A 2-man shelter should have a radius of 4 ft. and, therefore, the heap of snow should measure 12 ft. across and 6 ft. high.

■ Snow is collected and shovelled onto the mound. Do not pack it down in any way, by patting or tramping, since this produces uneven hardening. If necessary, the snow can be reshovelled to accelerate the process. The mound should be as close to a hemisphere as is possible to obtain.
■ When the mound has reached the required height (radius +2 ft.) it should be left for at

Fig. 66: A Soft Snow Mound Shelter

least one hour, preferably longer, to consolidate. Considerable shrinkage will take place overnight, even in cold weather and due allowance must be made for this.

■ After consolidation, dig into the centre of the mound and, leaving the marker in place, excavate round it. The finished product looks very much like an igloo, complete with door and air vent.

Snow Ball Shelter

In heavy damp snow it is possible to make various types of shelters from giant snow balls. These can be rolled together, preferably to a gathering area at the foot of a slope and then used as they stand, or cut into blocks to make a crude form of igloo.

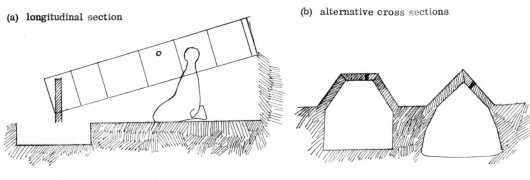

(a) longitudinal section

(b) alternative cross sections

Fig. 67: One man snow shelter

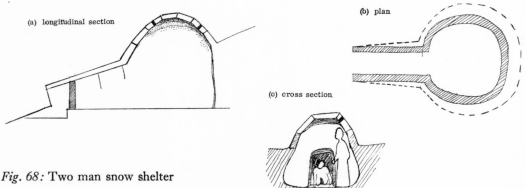

(a) longitudinal section

(b) plan

(c) cross section

Fig. 68: Two man snow shelter

The one and two man shelters shown in Figs. *67* and *68* can be built very quickly given reasonable snow and for this reason they are recommended as Emergency Shelters.

Combination Shelters

All sorts of combinations between the various types of shelters mentioned in this chapter are possible. The choice will be determined by the terrain and the snow condition. There is considerable scope for the fertile imagination in the ultimate design. However, speed, is often a vital safety factor and that must always be considered.

Perhaps the quickest of all snow shelters to build is the combined snow cave and igloo. The layout sketched below permits two people to dig side by side and without the disadvantage of working in a confined space. Excavation should be taken in the order 1 to 7 as indicated in the section and the blocks removed may be used later to build up the outer wall.

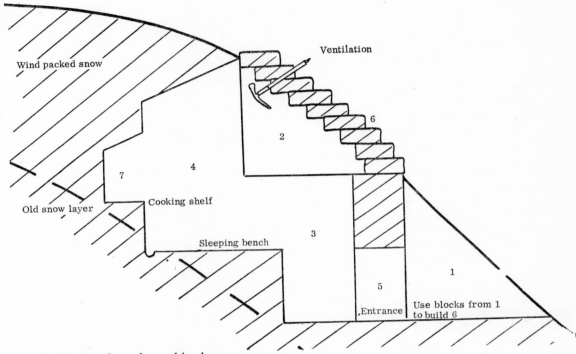

Fig. 69: Section through combined snow cave and igloo

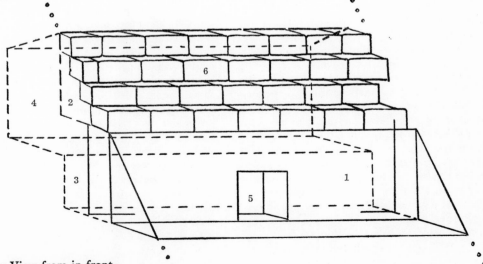

Fig. 70: View from in front

16 Frostbite

Definition

Frostbite is a condition which is fortunately relatively rare in this country. When it does occur it is usually associated with emergency situations involving forced bivouacs or with fractures or other injuries. Nevertheless it is very important to be able to give the right treatment in the field to avoid permanent damage or loss of tissue. The condition is closely related to Exposure, previously described (Chapters 6 and 7), since one of the body's reactions to general cooling is to reduce the supply of blood going to the extremities in order to conserve heat in the core. This is done at the expense of a greatly increased risk of frostbite since a sluggish circulation is stage one of the frostbite process. It is unusual, therefore, to have simply a frostbite problem to deal with. It must be appreciated that the local situation normally reflects a more serious general condition of body cooling and that both must be dealt with simultaneously. As in other things a knowledge of avoidance is paramount, coupled with early recognition and treatment before irrevocable damage is done. Recent work, particularly in America, has shed new light on the subject and brought significant improvements in the method of treatment.

Frostbite is the freezing or partial freezing of parts of the body, usually the face and extremities, the hands and feet. Provided the blood circulation to these parts is adequate and the tissue remains warm and nourished there is no danger of frostbite. Excessive surface cooling almost invariably exacerbated by faulty clothing or a condition of exhaustion, shock or general cooling of the whole body leads to a progressive reduction of circulation in the exposed part. Once this becomes negligible the tissue freezes. The initial stage of the process is known as 'frostnip'. This is speedily reversible provided action is taken in time. Keep a watch out for white nose, cheeks or ears on your companions and rewarm immediately. It is not possible to watch the hands and the feet as these are normally covered but cessation of feeling or even a feeling of warmth following cold, are danger signs which must not be ignored.

While it is fairly easy to rewarm the hands it takes a great deal of will power in a difficult situation to go to all the trouble of removing gaiters and boots to warm up the feet. However, if these warning signs are ignored true frostbite may be the result with a long and painful period of recovery and perhaps the risk of permanent tissue damage or even loss.

Treatment

'Frostnip' should be treated immediately by thawing the exposed part on some warm part of the anatomy. Fingers can be warmed under the armpit, ears by the hand, and feet on the belly of a companion. The important thing is to recognise this first stage of frostbite, *especially in the feet*, and rewarm immediately.

Frostbite, whether it be 'superficial', i.e. confined to the skin and surface tissue or 'deep', is a very serious condition.

The treatment, as for exposure, is one of rapid rewarming, but once rewarming has taken place the greatest of care is absolutely essential to protect the injury from further cooling or physical damage. For this reason it is best to head for home or for a base where adequate protection can be guaranteed. It is considerably less damaging to walk out on a frozen foot than a thawed one and in the likely circumstances a great deal safer for all concerned. In this country in almost every case the rule must be immediate evacuation to a place where professional medical help is available. In a situation where the victim is immobilised by other injuries and may have to wait some considerable time for rescue, treat for exposure by providing shelter, warmth and nourishment, but do not attempt to rewarm the frostbitten part by exercise or by any other means.

■ *Do not rub with snow* or for that matter anything else.

■ *Do not give alcohol.*

■ *Do not apply direct heat* from hot water bottle or stone to injury.

■ *Do not apply traction to fractures.*

This treatment or, more accurately, non-treatment ensures the maximum chance of recovery later. Fractures should be treated with a well padded splint and periodic checks made as to the state of the distal extremities. Shoes and boots must be removed and the foot padded gently with spare socks and sweaters and placed inside a rucksack.

It is highly unlikely that in this country it should ever be necessary to do more than is outlined above. The treatment at base would normally be supervised by a doctor or carried out in hospital. Experts on cold injury are agreed that immediate rapid rewarming for 20 minutes in a hot bath at 112°F offers the best hope of recovery and minimal loss of tissue. In the field when speedy evacuation is not possible, as on a major expedition abroad, this treatment should be administered at base camp.

Whether rewarming is induced or spontaneous, as could happen if the victim was evacuated to a warm tent at a low level or indeed if an early diagnosis of the injury had not been made, it is important to realise that further exercise or use of the frostbitten part is out of the question. In the case of a frostbitten foot the victim must be regarded as a stretcher case and evacuated accordingly. Everything must be done to prevent further damage or cooling. A dry, loose cotton wool dressing is all that is required after the injury has been gently cleaned by dabbing with warm (not hot) soapy water. Pads of wool may be required to separate the fingers or toes. A cage of some sort must then be improvised to prevent accidental damage and the pressure and drag of sleeping bag or blankets. On no account touch or prick blisters or interfere in any other way with the injury.

Prevention

Frostbite is inextricably related to the general degree of exposure of the whole body and the preventative measures previously recommended (see Chapter 6) to combat exposure are equally valid to give protection from frostbite. Basically a party that is fit, well fed, clad and watered, and in good spirits has little to fear. This assumes that the equipment and clothing worn, particularly on the hands and feet, will give adequate insulation from the cold. Boots must be roomy and allow for the wearing of one or two pairs of warm socks or stockings (loop stitched). A fitting which allows socks to wrinkle up under the heel or at the toes creates local pressure points which may become the focal point of frostbite injury. Do not wear wet socks or mitts, which incidentally are much superior to gloves as far as warmth is concerned, and carry spares of both.

In cold weather keep a watch on your companions' faces for any sign of frostnip (local pallor on nose, cheeks or ears). Stop and rewarm immediately. Rewarming the feet is a time-consuming business, but impress on everyone the importance of taking action in time. A feeling of numbness or even warmth following chill are warning signs which are ignored at your peril. Remember, too, that an exposed or injured person is much more liable to frostbite and, finally, that the 'freezing power' of the environment depends on wind as well as temperature (see Wind Chill chart, Fig. 17). The effect of a 40 m.p.h. wind at 20°F is exactly the same as that of a 2 m.p.h. wind at —40°F.

Snow Blindness

This has been referred to earlier when considering the effects of heat. Snow blindness is an extremely painful and debilitating condition brought about by exposure to intense ultra violet radiation. This radiation increases with altitude. Snow reflects about 90% of U.V. light, so that it is not enough merely to shield the eyes from direct sunlight. Goggles, or glasses, with all round protection are required, and in addition, they must filter at least 90% of this U.V. radiation. It is a common error to believe that eye protection is not required on dull, overcast days, and this has resulted in a number of unnecessary cases of snow blindness. In fact the eyes are particularly susceptible at this time because the pupils are dilated in response to the poor light, and therefore let in even more harmful radiation. The situation is further aggravated by internal reflection from the cloud base, so that the U.V. light echoes back and forward between the snow and the cloud, trapped, as it were, between two mirrors.

The condition varies in its severity, but can be recognised by bloodshot eyes and intense localised pain, often associated with headache. Apart from giving pain killing drugs there is little that can be done. The eyes should be bandaged and the patient rested in a darkened tent.

Readers are reminded that over-exposure to U.V. radiation can also result in painful and, occasionally, serious sunburn. Reliable preparations which effectively filter this should be applied to all exposed areas, particularly the nose and cheeks and the underside of the chin and ears.

17 Snow cover & avalanches

Avalanches are not peculiar to the Alpine countries. They occur with surprising frequency in Scotland. Care and judgement must be exercised at all times so that avalanche-prone slopes can be avoided. Above all, *be avalanche conscious.*

In Britain, to fall victim to an avalanche is an Act of God. In the Alps it is more commonly regarded as an act of folly. The truth, of course, lies somewhere in between, but there is a saying that most avalanche accidents are caused by their victims. To some extent at least, avalanches are predictable and though they may cause relatively few deaths in this country it is the duty of every mountain leader to acquaint himself with the fundamental causes and danger symptoms.

In recent years there has been a welcome increase in awareness among walkers and climbers of the frequency of avalanches in this country and the underlying causes of their development and release. This interest has been greatly stimulated by the publication of Colin Fraser's book 'The Avalanche Enigma' (Murray), a worthy successor to Seligman's 'Snow Structure and Ski Fields', for long the only authoritative work on this subject. It is only to be expected that the peculiarities of the British climate give rise to a peculiar type of avalanche or, more correctly, increase the frequency of certain types of avalanche. In assessing avalanche hazard in this country, then, it is important that these factors be borne in mind, though the actual process of build-up and release remains the same the world over.

Some examples of avalanches

In the winter of 1964/65 two young men were killed and five other persons injured by avalanches in the Cairngorms area alone. Many others were involved in incidents but were able to extricate themselves without injury. On Monday, 28th December, 1964, a party of four were descending the south west slope of Ben a Bhuird when suddenly and without warning a vast slab of snow broke off above them. Channelled by a shallow gully the debris swept down and buried three of the party. The fourth, separated from the slope by the gully, escaped and was able to raise the alarm in Braemar and return with the rescue party. One body was recovered that night and the search was only abandoned when lighting failed at 4 a.m. Incredibly a second victim was brought out alive though frostbitten when the search was resumed the next morning. The body of the fourth member was recovered later the same day.

On 10th March that same winter, a slab avalanche of Alpine proportions swept away three members of a party of eight descending from Coire an Lochain to the Lurchers gully. In this case the victims were at the top of the slope (Fig. 71). The fracture line literally split the party between the third and fourth man and they escaped a fall of over 900 feet with severe bruising. Had they been lower down they would almost certainly have been killed, since an estimated 100,000 tons of snow was involved in the slide.

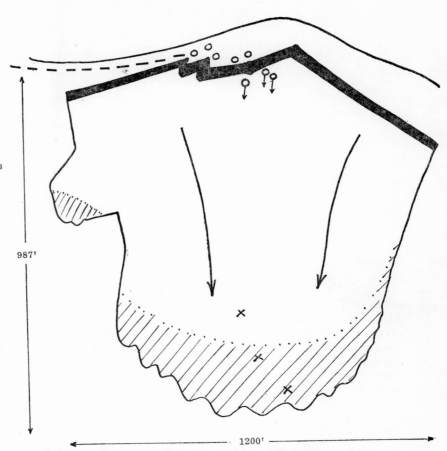

g. 71: Slab avalanche in ~~ire~~ an Lochain

~~ey:~~

— —   Track of party

~~o~~ o   Position of individuals before fracture

~~x~~ ×   position of victims

~~etails:~~

~~lab~~ thickness 9" – 2'0"

~~ean~~ angle of slope 28°:
~~aximum~~ angle of slope 37°

987'

1200'

A 900 ft. ride on the back of an avalanche is a daunting experience, yet it pales before the 1,800 ft. involuntary descent of the Central gully of Ben Laoigh by a well known Scottish mountaineer and party. They had in fact reached the summit by the same route and were starting the descent when the whole upper slope broke away below the cornice. They were carried down and deposited shaken, but none the worse, some distance below the start of the Gully proper. Before they had time to collect their wits a second avalanche, no doubt triggered by the first, came down upon them and carried three of the party a further few hundred feet. The leader, who had moved into the lee of a large rock to retrieve his axe, was mercifully spared this second round, the bulk of the snow passing over his head onto his friends below. The total damage after this affair was a lost rucksack, which was recovered six weeks later with a camera and film it contained, intact.

The snow cover

It has been said that no two snow crystals are ever exactly alike. Whether this is true or not, it is certainly the case that there is an almost infinite variety of shapes and forms based on the hexagonal system; stars, needles, plates, columns, grains and so on. The particular type of crystal formed is dependent on the atmospheric conditions at the time of formation. For example, grains and needles are associated with temperatures near the freezing point, while stellar crystals form at lower temperatures. Clearly, the physical properties of the individual crystals influence the behaviour of the whole snow layer. Some crystal types, such as needles or grains, readily form slabs while others, such as stars, tend to form loose deposits. Whatever the crystal form, the snow accumulates over the winter, each fall being represented by a more or less distinct layer. Just as the layering in a

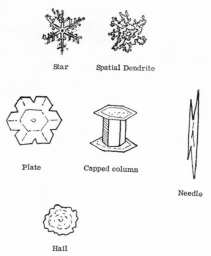

Fig. 72: Types of snow crystals

sedimentary rock reveals the history of its deposition so the layering of the snow cover tells the story of the winter storms. With the passage of time, the record becomes clouded by changes which take place within the snow cover.

From the moment of formation, snow crystals are subject to structural changes. The most important of these leads to a simplification of crystal structure, the rounding off of complex forms to produce a mass of isometric grains of great stability. This process is known as destructive metamorphism and its development is largely controlled by the temperature within the snow cover and by the pressure exerted by additional layers of snow. Increased temperature and pressure accelerate the process, while at low temperatures it is retarded and, in fact, stops altogether at −40°C. New snow may contain more than 90% air by volume, so it is hardly surprising that the most effective agent in promoting metamorphism is a dry wind, which can penetrate even thick masses of snow.

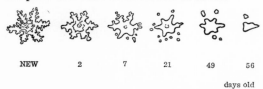

| NEW | 2 | 7 | 21 | 49 | 56 |

days old

Fig. 73: Destructive metamorphism in a crystal of new snow, maintained at a temperature of −5°c. The age of the crystal is shown in days below

The amount of heat stored in the ground after the summer is limited and in this country is certainly insufficient to melt the snow cover. Snow itself, being a poor conductor of heat, serves to insulate the ground and its own lower layers, from changes in surface temperature. The effect of this is to maintain the ground-snow interface at, or just below the freezing point, while the temperature of the surface layers fluctuate according to the environmental temperature. Thus, in a normal winter, there is a temperature gradient between the bottom and the top of the snow cover. The colder it is, the steeper the gradient.

Under its influence, water vapour moves upwards through the snow, from warmer to colder regions. This vapour migration causes a reduction in both the substance and the cohesion of the lower strata, so that the whole snow cover may be undermined from within. The vapour continues its upward passage and recrystallises at some more favourable locality. In the U.K., the outcome of this process is a general toughening of the upper layers at the expense of the lower, but in colder climates the recrystallisation is accelerated and a new crystal form appears. This is known as depth hoar, or cup crystal, from the appearance of these large and beautifully shaped crystals of ice in the lower regions of the snow cover.

The formation of depth hoar is favoured by prolonged cold conditions, particularly early in the winter when the snow cover is thin and

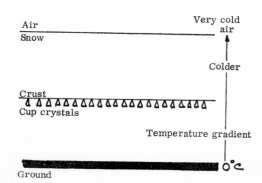

Fig. 74: Temperature gradient within the snow cover and the formation of depth hoar

(i) Poorly oriéntated crystals disappear

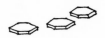

(ii) Prisms develop

(iii) Growth of cup crystals

(iv) Scaffold of depth hoar

Fig. 75: Formation of depth hoar

relatively vapour permeable. The danger lies in the fact that a layer of depth hoar forms an extremely fragile base for the layers above, rather like a stack of tumblers, each one balanced on the ones below. The danger is heightened by the fact that these changes take place at depth and are, therefore, likely to remain undetected unless the whole snow cover is examined in a snow pit. The surface layers, of course, may be perfectly stable and give no indication of the danger which lies below. Avalanches resulting from this gradual build-up are known as Climax Avalanches. Because of the relatively warm winter such avalanches are unlikely to occur in this country.

Snow avalanches are classified as loose or slab, according to the cohesion, or lack of it, displayed by the constituent crystals. In the case of loose snow avalanches, the individual crystals involved behave like dry sand tilted on a board. The avalanche, when it occurs, starts at a point, from the movement of a single grain and is cumulative, involving a rapidly increasing number of grains. Snow will normally slide in this way only when it is either very wet or very dry. Loose snow avalanches are, therefore, common during and immediately after, a fresh snow fall in calm conditions and also in the spring, when the snow becomes saturated with melt water. In the case of slab avalanches the crystals are bonded together to a greater or lesser degree so that the snow layer behaves as a cohesive mass. This cohesion may arise from a number of processes, including the normal process of destructive metamorphism. However, it is worth noting that an increase in cohesion is always associated with transport by wind and, in this country at least, slabs formed by wind action account for a high proportion of winter avalanches.

In addition to its internal cohesion which gives the snow its slab-like character, it is held in place by attachments on all sides and by adhesion to its underlayer, whether this is the ground or, as is more usual, another layer of snow. The strength of the slab is the sum of the strength of all the anchorages, and its stability depends on the relationship between that total strength and the stress which is applied to it. Where the stress exceeds the strength of all the anchorages, the slab will rupture and slide. Clearly, this situation can be reached, either by an increase in stress, such as an extra load of snow, or by a reduction in strength, due for example to lubrication of the under surface by melt water, or constructive metamorphism. The primary anchorage of a slab is to its underlayer and in any assessment of avalanche hazard it is the adhesion of one layer to another that demands special attention. Where adjoining layers show marked physical differences, e.g. a hard layer against a soft, adhesion is poor. When the layers are similar in character, or merge into one another, adhesion between them is good. A clue to the stability or otherwise of a slab is often given by small, harmless slides which fall away from the skis or boots. This is the basis of 'test ski-ing' which is carried out by the Ski Patrol to determine whether in fact, the snow will avalanche in a controlled situation. Failing evidence of this nature, a pit may be dug through the slab and the layers examined directly. In addition to looking at the contrasts between adjoining layers, any sharp discontinuities, particularly crusts, should be noted. These provide admirable sliding surfaces for the layers above and are a very common feature of the snow cover in Scotland.

For example – it is clear that dry new snow falling at low temperatures on top of a hard sun crust will have poor adhesion to the latter and that avalanche conditions can be expected. Wet new snow, on the other hand, subsequently frozen onto the same crust would have extremely good anchorage. Remember though, that thaw conditions, so common in this country, could later destroy the anchorage and, by accumulation of melt water on the crust, actually lubricate the sliding surface. A layer of light powder snow also provides an unstable base to a slab. This was the underlying cause of the avalanche in Coire Cas in 1968, which buried a party of nine climbers. The light snow falls of the previous day were followed by overnight drifting and slab formation in the Northern Coires. This slide was triggered by the victims themselves and on examination later it could be seen that the underlying powder layer had collapsed completely.

The converse, of course, also applies and the snow becomes more brittle as the temperature drops. The result of this is that cold snow is slow to adjust to stress and, therefore, tensions are built up within the snow cover which, if they are not released by avalanching, persist for some considerable time.

The conclusion we must draw from this is that in general, warm storms result in a short period of avalanche activity which quickly stabilises, while after cold storms this danger may persist for weeks.

So far, we have covered the attachment of one snow layer to another. The attachment of the whole snow cover to the ground and the nature and contours of the terrain is of equal importance. Obviously, irregularities and obstructions on the ground surface, such as boulders, trees, terracing, cross gullies and so on, tend to make for good anchorage, while fine scree, long grass and slabby glaciated rock surfaces tend to favour the avalanche situation. Particularly bad spots are often well known locally, e.g. the slabs below the cliffs of Coire an Lochain in the Cairngorms. *Find out where these places are and avoid them.* It must always be borne in mind that a heavy snowfall can nullify the holding properties of an irregular ground surface, by filling in all the holes and producing a smooth surface for the next fall.

```
                         Air      – 10°C

S U R F A C E   H O A R
▭▭▭▭▭▭▭▭▭▭▭▭▭

                         Snow     – 15°C



████████████████████

                         Ground
```

Fig. 76: Formation of surface hoar

Surface hoar is another lubricant to a slab avalanche. This is an atmospheric deposit of fragile, platey, crystals on the snow surface. Like depth hoar, these crystals have virtually no cohesion and keel over like a pack of cards when subjected to stress.

Normally, the snow cover adjusts to stress by creeping or sliding downhill. How much creep takes place depends on the plasticity of the snow, which in turn, is dependent on its temperature. Everyone is familiar with the deformation of snow on a roof top and how it slides and canopies over the eaves. The warmer it is the more rapid and extensive the creep.

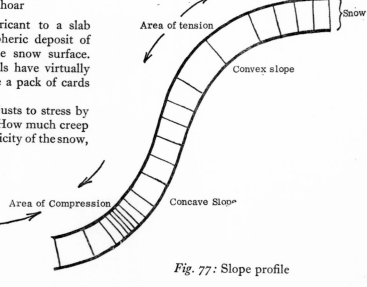

Fig. 77: Slope profile

All slopes of 22° and above should be regarded as suspect, though at angles above 50° it is unlikely that sufficient snow could accumulate to produce a serious slide. As well as the angle, the contours of a slope are important, particularly with regard to the line of fracture. Very often this is located along the line of maximum convexity, where tensile stresses are also at their maximum. Conversely, the concave part of a slope is an area of compression and therefore, one of relative stability.

Of all the other factors involved in the release of avalanches, the wind is perhaps the most significant. Not only does it result in the accumulation of large masses of snow on lee below the cornice is every bit as dangerous since it usually consists of deep wind slabbed snow at a high angle. The critical period is during, or immediately after the storm or wind which drifted the snow, until the snow settles and again, in the Spring, or after a prolonged thaw, when the cornice itself becomes exceedingly dangerous.

It is always as well to give a cornice a wide berth. The likelihood is that it will fracture along the shortest line between the snow surface and the ridge below, but all too often it takes a large piece of the opposing face with it. The critical angle for cornice formation is not to be found on the lee side as you might expect,

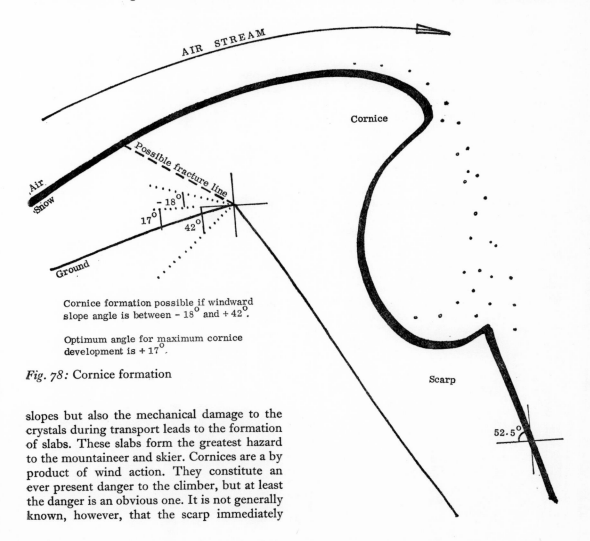

Cornice formation possible if windward slope angle is between − 18° and + 42°.

Optimum angle for maximum cornice development is + 17°.

Fig. 78: Cornice formation

slopes but also the mechanical damage to the crystals during transport leads to the formation of slabs. These slabs form the greatest hazard to the mountaineer and skier. Cornices are a by product of wind action. They constitute an ever present danger to the climber, but at least the danger is an obvious one. It is not generally known, however, that the scarp immediately but on the windward slope, 17° being the optimum angle, while −18° and 42° are the limits on either side. Irrespective of the angle of the lee slope, the scarp will always tend to build itself up to an angle of 52½°.

18 The classification of avalanches

It should by now be clear that it is just not possible to classify avalanches by any one criterion. There are many variations and indeed an infinite range within each variation, as between 'wet' and 'dry'. Again, what may start as one type of avalanche may develop into a more complex form. A fall of ice seracs could trigger off a wind slab which in turn could pulverise into a dry powder avalanche, part airborne and part flowing. There is, however, a need for some quick descriptive, if scientifically inexact, classification. The system generally accepted is that proposed by the Swiss Snow and Avalanche Research Institute illustrated by Fig. 79. This is based on a five-point system. A 6th criterion is sometimes added to the list, namely, the triggering mechanism. This may be *external* if the source of the disturbance which causes release is outside the snow cover. Examples of this are the collapse of a cornice, a sonic boom, or, more frequently, the disturbance caused by the climbers or skiers themselves. Or, it can be *internal* as is the case when the snow cover is overloaded with fresh snow, or when there is a reduction in the strength of a snow layer brought about, perhaps, by the gradual accumulation of depth hoar.

In conclusion let us look at our winter weather pattern and see how it affects the frequency and type of avalanche to be expected in this country.

In the first place we have a relatively low snow fall; this means that avalanches are considerably less frequent and less widespread in their occurrence. Add to this the shorter slope length and the fact that falls in excess of two feet are exceedingly rare and you have a situation which precludes the possibility of devastating slides on an Alpine scale.

Nevertheless there are factors which operate against the foregoing and the most important of these is wind. The snow cover may be slight but the ubiquitous wind redistributes it into the gullies and on to the lee slope where it can accumulate to enormous depths in thick snow cushions or in the sinister garb of wind slab. However, the field is narrowed thereby and these places can be avoided. If the last heavy snowfall came on a south west wind then keep clear of all north east facing slopes until conditions have stabilised. In particular, beware of soft slab avalanches in these areas during or immediately after a storm and hard slab avalanches over a longer period, especially when conditions remain cold.

Rapid changes in the weather pattern are characteristic of the United Kingdom, with relatively high average winter temperatures with the freezing level bobbing up and down our mountain sides with astonishing rapidity. This not only hinders the accumulation of snow but also tends to have a settling effect in that it favours the process of destructive metamorphism. At the same time it encourages the development of crust layers. These crusts may be produced by wind or sun or by melting and refreezing. But whatever the cause, they are a potential source of danger when covered by further snow falls. Wind transported snow, or dry new snow, falling on such crusts gives rise to avalanche conditions.

Rain can fall at any time throughout the winter. It has little effect on spring snow, but it can give rise to dangerous conditions earlier in the year where heavy slabs of snow are poorly anchored to the underlayer. A feature of our winter is the protracted spring when well consolidated sugary snow lingers on the tops and

Criterion	Either	Or
1. Type of break	Loose 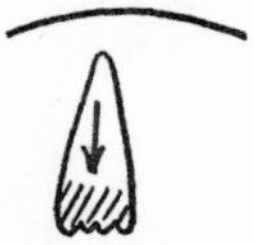	Slab 
2. Sliding surface	Full depth 	Surface 
3. Humidity	Dry	Wet
4. Form of break	Unconfined 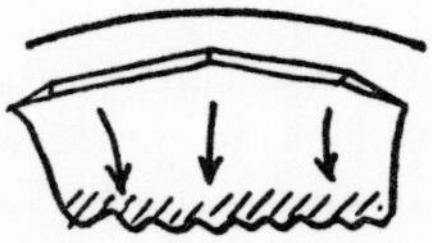	Channelled 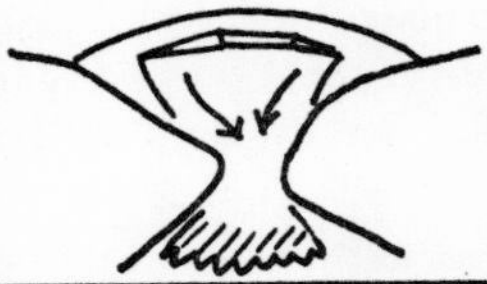
5. Movement	Airborne 	Flowing 

Fig. 79: The classification of avalanches

in the gullies. Wet snow avalanches are uncommon since by this time the snow is well consolidated and later falls are shallow and rarely subjected to the drastic thaws of the Alpine spring. The risk at this time of year is not so much from wet snow as from old snow whose attachment to the ground has been undermined by percolating water. The paths of these spring avalanches are often well known locally where some peculiarity of the ground favours their release. For instance the avalanche of old snow in Coire an Lochain in the Cairngorms takes place every year in early May or thereabouts and is caused by the action of water in breaking the bond between the great snow mass (up to 25 feet thick) and the 600 feet sheet of smooth granite slabs below.

Powder

Occurrence	*Characteristics*	*Danger Signs*
Dominant Winter type in cold, dry conditions. Not common in U.K.	Starts silently as loose snow avalanche, i.e. it starts from a single point and not as a slab.	Any fall of dry new snow in excess of 9″, or area of thick local accumulation.
On slopes of 22° or more, the higher the altitude the greater and more prolonged the risk.	May be flowing, airborne or a combination of the two. The airborne form is the more devastating.	Where dry new snow falls on crust, be it caused by wind, sun or frozen wet snow.
North and East facing slopes may remain avalanche prone for weeks till settled.	Many achieve great speed and turbulence.	A sudden rise in temperature after a fall.
South facing slopes will settle after two or three days of fine weather.	Preceded and accompanied by a powerful blast.	Sunballs. Snowballs trickling down a slope under the melting action of the sun on the surface layer.

Soft slab

The most common form of avalanche in Scotland.	Initial breakaway as a slab with a distinct fracture wall.	Any snow storm when there is a rapid accumulation of snow (1″ per hour or more).
Widespread danger during and immediately after snow-storms. May last several days if cold.	Usually silent. Slab breaks up and pulverised leaving few distinct blocks in the debris.	Slabs in excess of 10″ thick are dangerous. An underlayer of powder snow or crust offers poor anchorage.
Often associated with wind in which case lee slopes are particularly prone to avalanche.	Surface, flowing.	Storms which start cold and finish warm are more likely to produce avalanching than the reverse conditions.
		Some crystal forms, such as needles and granular snow, tend to produce slabs.

Hard slabs

'Hard slab' is the most dangerous type of avalanche because its firmness encourages a false sense of security.	Extensive clean fracture line, usually released with loud report. Initial slabs of snow break up, but do not pulverise.	Very difficult to recognise. The uncovered surface has a chalky, non-reflective appearance and is very hard.
Associated with snow transport and packing by strong, cold winds and therefore common on lee slopes at high altitude.	Devastating.	Sudden subsidence with booming noise on level ground is one of the few diagnostic signs.
Associated also with weak underlayer of depth hoar, or		A cold and windy weather history.

Occurrence	Characteristics	Danger Signs
occasionally powder snow. There may even be a thin space below the slab where this underlayer has contracted away due to settling.		Any obvious signs of wind action, such as sastrugi. A sudden fall in temperature may be the trigger. Check underlayers in a snow pit and remember that a slab may lie buried beneath layers of apparently safe snow.

Climax

As its name suggests, this type of avalanche is the result of a prolonged build-up. The most common cause is overloading by fresh snow falls, of a deep seated weaker stratum in the snow cover, usually depth hoar. It is therefore associated with a prolonged early cold spell. Unrecorded in Scotland.	Usually slab in form and involving the whole snow cover down to the ground. Tend to be large and devastating.	No surface signs and can only be recognised by digging a snow pit and by examining the weather history for the season.

Wet

Dominant Spring type. Larger ones follow well defined tracks. Fall on relatively shallow gradients at all altitudes in thaw conditions. Early afternoon critical time in fair weather. May start below rocks which cause local thawing.	Loose or slab in form, with characteristic 'ruffled carpet' start. Flowing and develops roar similar to a waterfall. Contains snow boulders. Moves relatively slowly and can therefore sometimes be outrun by a competent skier. Debris consolidates under great pressure and freezes instantly. Very destructive.	Sudden rise in temperature especially in humid and over-cast conditions and following heavy fall of snow. Wet snowfalls, rain and warm wet winds. Sticky snow. Large snowballs penetrating deep into cover. Cracks and rifts in the snow cover. Slopes scarred by previous avalanches. Depth hoar layers will be further weakened.

Avalanche Protection – a summary

■ *Most avalanche accidents are caused by their victims. Keep high and on the ridges and avoid being the trigger which releases a slide.*

■ *Keep clear of accumulation areas during and immediately after a snow storm.*

■ *Lee slopes are particularly prone to soft slab avalanches.*

■ *Never go alone.*

■ *Never expose more than one of the party to risk at any given moment.*

■ *Do not assume that the passage of another party is proof that a slope is safe.*

■ *Avoid cornices and the slopes below them.*

■ *Fracture commonly takes place on the convex part of a slope.*

■ *The most dangerous slope angles are between 30° and 45°.*

■ *Avalanche slopes which run out into gullies where the debris can pile up are especially dangerous.*

■ *Thin forest makes poor protection.*

■ *Consult local expert advice and obey all avalanche warning notices.*

■ *Carry avalanche cords and trail at all danger spots.*

■ *Carry first aid kit and basic rescue equipment in the party.*

■ *Know how to improvise a rope or ski stretcher.*

■ *Find out the recent weather history.*

■ *Be on the look out for warning signs, such as booming of snow, heavy sun-balling, fresh avalanche tracks, cracks in the snow when weighted, mini avalanches from the boots or skis.*

■ *Low temperatures prolong avalanche risk.*

■ *A sudden increase in temperature after snowfall, especially with a dry wind, creates avalanche danger.*

■ *Rain on unconsolidated snow gives rise to wet avalanches, especially where the underlayer offers poor attachment.*

■ *Powder avalanches are rare in Scotland, but occasionally fall after one foot or more of new snow in cold weather. Slopes take 2 – 3 days to settle and longer if cold and out of the sun.*

■ *The attachment of snow layers to each other is of fundamental importance. Assess this by digging a small pit or by probing with axe or ski stick. Adjoining layers which differ markedly in hardness are likely to be poorly attached to each other. Note particularly any weak layers and crusts.*

■ *The deeper the snow, the greater the danger. An accumulation rate in excess of 1″ per hour leads to avalanche hazard.*

19 Avalanche search and rescue

Speed is of paramount importance in any avalanche search operation. The chances of survival are greatly reduced as the burial time increases. Few victims are brought out alive after two hours or more in the snow. See Fig. 80 showing graph of survival times. The operation may be considered in three phases:

■ a preliminary search by the survivors of the avalanche.

■ an advance party search carried out with the men and equipment that can be got to the site without delay.

■ a systematic search using probes, dogs and other methods of detection.

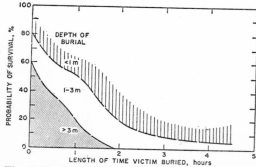

Fig. 80: Probability of survival for avalanche victims as a function of time, showing also the effect of depth of burial. In Switzerland, the survival rate for completely buried victims is 19%. (From a study of avalanche accidents by de Quervain).

Search by survivors

It is of vital importance that the position of the victims when engulfed and when last seen be marked on the ground. The line connecting these two points acts as a pointer to the likely burial area. This area and indeed the whole of the debris should be examined as closely as time permits for any sign of the victim, his clothing or equipment. A reversed ski stick or a stick with the basket removed makes a simple probe to test likely spots.

Obviously the amount of time devoted to this preliminary search depends on the location of the accident and the number of survivors. However, this surface search is absolutely essential and half an hour to an hour is suggested as being of the right order.

Advance party search

An advance party must be sent immediately and with all speed to the site of the avalanche. They should take with them only what is immediately available in the form of first aid, shovels and sounding rods or sticks. It is the job of this party to follow up the preliminary search and concentrate their attention on the most likely area of debris.

Systematic search

A great many people may be involved in this phase and a high degree of accuracy and co-ordination is essential. For these reasons the search must be conducted with military precision and must be under the direct control of one man.

In spite of all the scientific advances in this field the two oldest methods of search remain the most effective, namely the use of sounding rods or probes and the use of dogs.

Use of Sounding Rods

These come in a variety of forms but are normally jointed metal rods up to 12 ft. in length. The rescuers are arranged in an extended line across the debris and advance up the slope probing at set intervals and to a set depth. An area once searched in this way should be clearly marked with flags or sticks.

It is normal to probe to a depth of 6 ft. even although the depth of the debris may be considerably greater. The saving in time far outweighs the slim chance of finding a victim alive at a greater depth. Even with a team of 20–30 people the business of probing takes a very long time and here again a saving can be made by adopting a wide spacing between probes. Rescuers stand with their feet 20 inches apart and separated from their neighbours' feet by a distance of 10 inches.

For coarse probing the rods are driven in between the feet. The whole line then advances by one 2 ft. pace and the process is repeated. In this way a 2 ft. square grid is built up.

For fine probing the rods are driven in at both toes and also centrally. The line then advances by 1 ft. and the process is repeated. In this way a 1 ft. grid is built up.

The great disadvantage of sounding, effective though it is, is the length of time it takes to cover the ground, even with large numbers of rescuers. It is for this reason that a well trained dog is worth its weight in gold for it can search a given area in a tenth of the time that it would take a team of 20 men.

Use of Avalanche Trained Dogs

Details of the Search and Rescue Dog Association have been given on page 59.

If dogs are to be used at all they should be brought to the site of the accident as soon as possible. There is no reason why the search should be delayed till their arrival, provided the area is cleared 10–15 minutes before they are set to work. The rescuers must of course move off down-wind of the area.

Trenching

If these methods fail to locate the victim trenches must be dug into the debris. These trenches should be approximately 1 yard wide and spaced at intervals of 3 yards. The walls of the trenches should then be probed horizontally.

Other Methods

Many other ingenious methods of detection have been devised. They can be divided roughly into those which require the victim to carry some device such as a VHF transmitter or a magnetic disc and those which depend on some natural function or property of the body. The latter offer the best hope for development since it is always difficult to persuade people to carry extra equipment, no matter how compact. However, for organised groups and search parties miniature electronic devices are now available which can be located accurately within a matter of minutes from a range of about 100 feet.

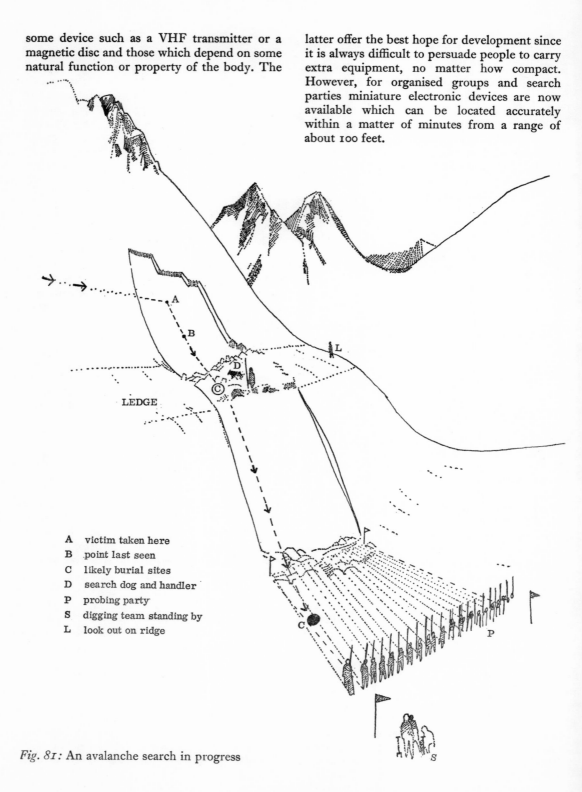

A   victim taken here
B   point last seen
C   likely burial sites
D   search dog and handler
P   probing party
S   digging team standing by
L   look out on ridge

Fig. 81: An avalanche search in progress

First Aid

The victim may be suffering from suffocation, shock, exposure, frostbite and other mechanical injuries to the body. If necessary, mouth-to-mouth resuscitation and/or external cardiac massage should be given immediately (remember that the mouth is likely to be full of snow). Great care should be exercised in taking the victim out of the snow so as not to aggravate any injuries. He should be placed on a casualty bag in the head-low position and the treatment continued as discussed in Chapter 7 and Chapter 16.

What to do if caught in an avalanche

This is the sort of advice which is easy to give but which may be quite impossible to follow. However, it is the distillation of the experience of many victims over a period of years. There are of course a number of physical variables, to say nothing of human ones, and the best course of action depends to a large extent on them. For instance, what may be a number one priority in a powder snow avalanche may be of little importance in a slab one.

■ Remove rucksack and skis (these should already be in the quick release position if there is any risk of avalanche). A good skier may of course be able to schuss out of danger.

■ Make a quick assessment of the avalanche; whether you are at the top, bottom, middle, or to one side; what type it is (wet, dry, etc.) and where your best line of escape lies. There may be a handy crevasse nearby!

■ Delay your departure as long as possible. The more you let past you at the start the less will bury you at the finish.

■ It may be advantageous to work out to the side of the avalanche.

■ If swimming movements are possible, then a sort of double-action back stroke seems to be the most effective, with the back to the force of the avalanche and the head up. Obviously, if you are in danger of being struck by blocks and slabs of snow then your arms will have to be used to protect your head and face. There is no cut and dried procedure here – ride it out as best you can and save your great effort for the last seconds.

■ Keep your mouth shut! In a powder avalanche cover the mouth and nose with a handkerchief or other piece of clothing (the top of a sweater or anorak).

■ A supreme effort should be made in the last few seconds as the avalanche loses its momentum and begins to settle. Two things are paramount: an air space; and a position as near to the surface as possible. The chances of survival are greatly reduced if buried deep (4 ft. plus).

■ Don't panic!

When crossing suspected avalanche slope

remember to . . .

■ Loosen your ski bindings and safety straps and to take your hands out of stick straps.

■ Loosen rucksack straps and be prepared to shed any other impedimenta.

■ Secure your anorak hood over your mouth and nose if possible.

■ Trail an avalanche cord. This is a 50 ft. length of brightly coloured nylon tied to the waist at one end and left to trail behind you on the snow. Should you be taken by an avalanche it is possible that some part of this light cord will be thrown up on the surface, even if you are not. The cord has metal tags crimped on at 2 metre intervals with an arrow and the number of metres to the end of the cord (in the direction of the arrow) marked on. Just make sure you tie on to the right end of the cord!

■ Go down on foot rather than ski.

■ Go straight down rather than make a descending traverse.

■ Cross high and if possible on a concave slope. The latter is generally more stable than other slopes and the higher you are the less chance there is of being buried.

■ Cross one at a time. Never assume that the passage of another party is proof that the slope is safe. They may well be the first pressure on the trigger.

BOOKS TO READ

Department of Agriculture Handbook No. 194. 'Snow Avalanches', U.S. Government Printing Office.

Snow Structure and Ski Fields, by Seligman.
*Avalanche Enigma, by Colin Fraser (Murray).
The Avalanche Hunters by Montgomery Atwater.
Handbook of Ski Mountaineering, by D. R. Brower, Sierra Club, San Francisco.
Mountaineering – The Freedom of the Hills, by Mountaineers Incorporated.
Snow and its Metamorphosis, by Snow, Ice and Permafrost Research Establishment, translation No. 14. U.S. Army Corps of Engineers.
*The ABC of Avalanche Safety – E. La Chapelle, Colorado Outdoor Sports Co., Denver, Colorado. Available Glenmore Lodge.
Ski Touring and Glacier Ski-ing, Ski Club of Great Britain, 118 Eaton Square, London, S.W.1.
*Recommended

FILMS TO SEE
Dial Double One, Petroleum Films Bureau, 4 Brook Street, London, W.1.
Avalanche Control, Regional Office, Forest Service, U.S. Department of Agriculture.

Appendix W: Sample theory papers

Appendix W1

Scottish Mountain Leadership Certificate (Winter) Mountaineering

1 Wool is brushed so that
(a) It has a better finish
(b) It wears well
(c) Does not collect dirt
(d) Allows the skin to breath
(e) Traps more air
Which is the correct answer?
2 Box quilting
(a) Has a double layer
(b) Has less feathers
(c) Is cheaper
(d) Has overlapping seams
(e) Avoids heat loss at seams
Which is correct?
3 How are seams of waterproof clothing made waterproof? (a), (b).
4 Which is the more durable proofing: (a) Neoprene, (b) Polyurethene?
5 What is the danger of P.V.C. garments in winter?
6 A winter climbing boot should have a rigid sole. True or false?
7 Instep crampons are adequate for most winter mountaineering situations in the Cairngorms. True or false?
8 What is the danger of using nylon overmitts with an ice axe?
9 What is the difference between gaiters and stop tout?
10 Do you regard snow gaiters as essential winter equipment?
11 What is the reply to the Alpine distress signal?
12 What is the term given to iced rock?
13 When should morphine not be given? (a), (b).
14 What is the percentage of body heat loss from the exposed head?
15 Of what mountaineering use are snowballs?
16 What is missing from the following route card?
Date, Leader, Number and names and addresses of Party, Depart and Return times, Route time, Distance/Bearings/Rests/Stops.
17 What is Dayglo?
18 What are the following: Damart, Borg, Thermawear, Polar Suit?
19 Where are the RAF Rescue Teams in Scotland based, (a), (b).
20 What is a pied d'elephant?
21 What ice piton/screw would you use on hard brittle ice?
22 What is the danger of crampons in soft snow?
23 What is the danger of crampons worn with long trousers?
24 When ice axe braking with crampons on, what must you do?
25 Why carry out the manoeuvre in Q. 24?
26 Where do you normally belay in a snow gully?
27 What is the best belay: ice bollard, snow mushroom, deadman, rock spike, two linked ice pegs?
28 What posture would you adopt in an emergency bivouac to conserve heat?
29 You have snow holes which are drifting up. What two steps do you take to safeguard the party?
30 When you leave your snowhole and expect to return, what must you do; (a), (b).
31 Your end man goes missing in a white out. What first course of action do you take after finding out he has not been seen for 3 minutes?
32 What are the *two* dangers of a convex slope?
33 How would you abseil out of a snow gully leaving no gear behind?
34 You have lost your snow goggles on a sunny day with full snow cover. How would you improvise to protect your eyes?
35 How do you remove snow sticking to your crampons?
36 When step cutting on ice without crampons, how should the steps be cut?
37 What is the safest way to descend steep snow – facing out, facing sideways, facing in?
38 What do the following initials stand for: S.M.C., M.C.S., M.R.C.S?

39 Straight forward, average angled snow gullies, generally showing no pitches under adequate snow cover. They may however present cornice difficulty. What grade is this?

40 What is a Leeper?

41 What is spindrift?

42 What is a bellows tongue?

Appendix W2
Scottish Mountain Leadership Certificate (Winter) Snow and Avalanche

1 Rime ice is found on the (a) windward, (b) lee side of boulders exposed to super cooled water droplets.

2 Hard wind slab is found on the (a) windward, (b) lee slopes, (c) ridge crest, (d) frost hollows, (e) both lee and windward slopes.

3 Small channels and ridges carved out of the snow surface are known as . . .?

4 The risk of powder snow avalanche is greatest (a) after, (b) during a snow fall?

5 How is Verglas formed, i.e. under what conditions is it formed?

6 During periods of very severe frosts sublimation and recrystalisation takes place in the snow layers. What are the crystals called?

7 What is the effect of the above crystals on the anchorage of the snow layers?

8 What forms on cold snow when warmer moist air is in contact with its surface?

9 Does 8 form a good adhesive base for the subsequent snow falls?

10 In a convex/concave snow slope which area is (a) least stable, (b) most stable?

11 What is nevé?

12 What is randkluft?

13 How would you ascertain in the field the condition of a snow slope which you had to cross, i.e. evaluate the avalanche risk?

14 A full depth avalanche is more common on what three surfaces, (a), (b), (c).

15 Why are slopes above 50° less of an avalanche hazard?

16 Below what angle may slopes seldom avalanche/slide?

17 In spring during clear weather when is the best time to cross an avalanche slope?

18 What determines when it will be safe to travel after a severe snow storm?

19 Where would you cross an avalanche prone slope? (a), (b).

20 What type of avalanche can occur at any time?

21 What is the normal angle of a scarp slope?

22 Where will you find a scarp slope?

23 What will wind ripples or waves on the snow indicate?

24 What are cracks or rifts in the snow cover danger signs of?

25 What are large snow balls penetrating deep into snow cover and sticky snow danger signs of?

26 Sunballs – snowballs trickling down a slope under the melting action of the sun on the surface layer are a danger sign of?

27 Is survival time under wet snow longer or shorter than under dry snow?

28 If you are the solitary witness of an avalanche would you (a) attempt to search for victims, (b) go for help immediately for probes and shovels?

29 Which snow has a chalky, non-reflective appearance and may have a deceptively firm appearance?

30 What information would you ask the witness of an avalanche, assuming one person had been avalanched and he has no avalanche cord?

31 What is the normal depth of probing?

32 What is the grid distance of a fine probe?

33 What is the grid distance of a coarse probe?

34 What traditional method is more effective than probing?

35 If 33 and 34 fail to find the victim, what is the last used search technique?

36 What slopes will tend to settle more quickly in fine weather?

37 Why?

38 After what period is the survival rate of avalanche victims very low? 10 minutes, 30 minutes, 2 hours.

39 How long is an avalanche cord?

40 When would you use it?

41 Does snow transmit sound well?

42 Does the presence of a small amount of water in snow increase or decrease its cohesion?

43 Snow is falling with a N.W. wind. Where will large accumulations of snow form?

44 What is the optimum angle of the windward slope for cornice formation?

45 Cornice formation is possible when the windward slope angle is between − 18° and ....?